SOLUTIONS MANUAL AND STUDY GUIDE

Fundamentals of Futures and Options Markets

Ninth Edition

John C. Hull

Maple Financial Group Professor of
Derivatives and Risk Management
Joseph L. Rotman School of Management
University of Toronto

Sponsoring Editor: Neeraj Bhalla

Project Manager: Alison Kalil

Cover Art: ktsdesign/Fotolia

ISBN-10: 0-13-408365-2

ISBN-13: 978-0-13-408365-0

PEARSON

Contents

Preface

This book contains answers to the practice questions that appear at the ends of chapters in my book *Fundamentals of Futures and Options Markets*, 9th edition. The questions have been designed to help readers study on their own and test their understanding of the material. They range from quick checks on whether a key point is understood to much more challenging applications of analytical techniques. To maximize the benefits from this book readers are urged to sketch out their own answers before consulting mine.

For each chapter, this manual includes a summary of the main points together with suggestions of ways readers should approach studying the material. You should find these summaries useful both when you first cover the material in a chapter and when you are studying for an exam.

I welcome comments on either *Fundamentals of Futures and Options Markets*, 9th edition, or this book. My e-mail address is hull@rotman.utoronto.ca

John C. Hull
Joseph L. Rotman School of Management
University of Toronto

CHAPTER 1
Introduction

This chapter introduces futures, forward, and option contracts and explains the traders that use them. If you already know how these contracts work, you will not have to spend too much time on this chapter. Note that Chapter 1 does not distinguish between futures and forward contracts. Both are agreements to buy or sell an asset at a certain time in the future for a certain price. It is Chapter 2 that covers the daily settlement feature of futures contracts and itemizes the differences between the two types of contract.

Make sure you understand the key difference between futures/forwards and options. Futures and forwards are obligations to enter into a transaction in the future. An option is the right to enter into a transaction in the future. A futures or forward contract may prove to be an asset or a liability (depending on how the price of the underlying asset evolves). An option is always an asset to the buyer of the option and a liability to the seller of the option. It costs money (the option premium) to purchase an option. There is no cost (except for margin/collateral requirements which are discussed in Chapter 2) when a futures or forward contract is entered into. Table 1.1 shows forward foreign exchange quotes. Tables 1.2 and 1.3 show the prices of options on Google. Make sure you understand what the numbers in these tables mean and how the profit diagrams in Figure 1.3 are constructed.

The distinction between over-the-counter and exchange-traded markets is important. As Figure 1.2 indicates, the OTC market was about ten times the size of the exchange-traded market at the end of 2014. Exchange-traded markets are markets where the contracts are defined by an exchange such as the CME Group. How trading is done, how payments flow from one side to the other, and so on is determined by the exchange. A key point is that the exchange (or, strictly speaking, the exchange clearing house) stands between the two sides and organizes trading so that there is virtually no credit risk.

The over-the-counter (OTC) market is primarily a market between financial institutions, non-financial corporations, and fund managers. Traditionally, OTC market participants have communicated and agreed on trades by phone or electronically. An exchange is not involved. However, as a result of regulatory initiatives, the OTC market is becoming more like the exchange-traded market. Three important regulatory initiatives are:

1. Standard OTC derivatives between financial institutions in the U.S. must whenever possible be traded by swap execution facilities. These are platforms where market participants can post bid and offer quotes and where they can do a trade by accepting the bid or offer quote of another market participant.
2. Central clearing parties must be used for standard OTC derivatives between financial institutions. Their role is to stand between the two sides in the same way that the exchange clearing house does in the exchange-traded market.
3. All trades must be reported to a central registry.

The chapter identifies the three main types of trader that use forward, futures, and option markets. *Hedgers* use the markets to reduce their risk exposure to a market variable such as an exchange rate, a commodity price, or an interest rate. *Speculators* use the market to take a position on the future direction of a market variable. *Arbitrageurs* attempt to lock in a riskless profit by simultaneously entering into transactions in two or more markets. The chapter gives examples of the activities of the three types of traders. Hedge funds (see Business Snapshot 1.3) use derivatives for all three purposes. As the SocGen example (Business Snapshot 1.4) shows, one of the dangers in derivatives markets is that a trader will use derivatives for unauthorized speculation and lose a lot of money before the trader's employer finds out what is going on.

Answers to Practice Questions

Problem 1.8.
Suppose you own 5,000 shares that are worth $25 each. How can put options be used to provide you with insurance against a decline in the value of your holding over the next four months?

You should buy 50 put option contracts (each on 100 shares) with a strike price of $25 and an expiration date in four months. If at the end of four months the stock price proves to be less than $25, you can exercise the options and sell the shares for $25 each.

Problem 1.9.
A stock when it is first issued provides funds for a company. Is the same true of an exchange-traded stock option? Discuss.

An exchange-traded stock option provides no funds for the company. It is a security sold by one investor to another. The company is not involved. By contrast, a stock when it is first issued is sold by the company to investors and does provide funds for the company.

Problem 1.10.
Explain why a futures contract can be used for either speculation or hedging.

If an investor has an exposure to the price of an asset, he or she can hedge with futures contracts. If the investor will gain when the price decreases and lose when the price increases, a long futures position will hedge the risk. If the investor will lose when the price decreases and gain when the price increases, a short futures position will hedge the risk. Thus either a long or a short futures position can be entered into for hedging purposes.
If the investor has no exposure to the price of the underlying asset, entering into a futures contract is speculation. If the investor takes a long position, he or she gains when the asset's price increases and loses when it decreases. If the investor takes a short position, he or she loses when the asset's price increases and gains when it decreases.

Problem 1.11.
A cattle farmer expects to have 120,000 pounds of live cattle to sell in three months. The live-cattle futures contract on the Chicago Mercantile Exchange is for the delivery of 40,000 pounds of cattle. How can the farmer use the contract for hedging? From the farmer's viewpoint, what are the pros and cons of hedging?

The farmer can short 3 contracts that have 3 months to maturity. If the price of cattle falls, the gain on the futures contract will offset the loss on the sale of the cattle. If the price of cattle rises, the gain on the sale of the cattle will be offset by the loss on the futures contract. Using futures contracts to hedge has the advantage that it can greatly reduce the uncertainty about the price that will be received for the cattle. Its disadvantage is that the farmer no longer gains from favorable movements in cattle prices.

Problem 1.12.
It is July 2016. A mining company has just discovered a small deposit of gold. It will take six months to construct the mine. The gold will then be extracted on a more or less continuous basis for one year. Futures contracts on gold are available on the New York Mercantile Exchange. There are delivery months every two months from August 2016 to December 2017. Each contract is for the delivery of 100 ounces. Discuss how the mining company might use futures markets for hedging.

The mining company can estimate its production on a month by month basis. It can then short futures contracts to lock in the price received for the gold. For example, if a total of 3,000 ounces are expected to be produced in September 2017 and October 2017, the price received for this production can be hedged by shorting a total of 30 October 2017 contracts.

Problem 1.13.
Suppose that a March call option on a stock with a strike price of $50 costs $2.50 and is held until March. Under what circumstances will the holder of the option make a gain? Under what circumstances will the option be exercised? Draw a diagram showing how the profit on a long position in the option depends on the stock price at the maturity of the option.

The holder of the option will gain if the price of the stock is above $52.50 in March. (This ignores the time value of money.) The option will be exercised if the price of the stock is above $50.00 in March. The profit as a function of the stock price is shown in Figure S1.1.

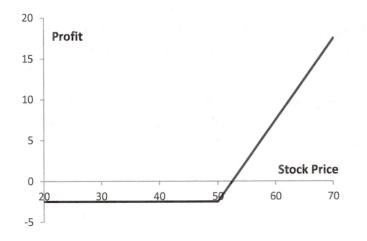

Figure S1.1   Profit from long position in Problem 1.13

3

Problem 1.14.

Suppose that a June put option on a stock with a strike price of $60 costs $4 and is held until June. Under what circumstances will the holder of the option make a gain? Under what circumstances will the option be exercised? Draw a diagram showing how the profit on a short position in the option depends on the stock price at the maturity of the option.

The seller of the option will lose if the price of the stock is below $56.00 in June. (This ignores the time value of money.) The option will be exercised if the price of the stock is below $60.00 in June. The profit as a function of the stock price is shown in Figure S1.2.

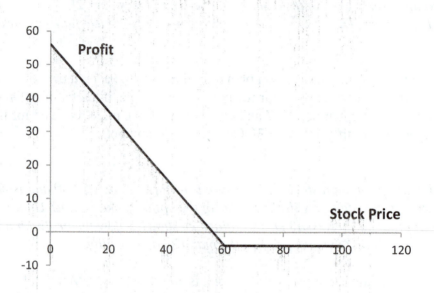

Figure S1.2   Profit from short position in Problem 1.14

Problem 1.15.

It is May and a trader writes a September call option with a strike price of $20. The stock price is $18, and the option price is $2. Describe the investor's cash flows if the option is held until September and the stock price is $25 at this time.

The trader has an inflow of $2 in May and an outflow of $5 in September. The $2 is the cash received from the sale of the option. The $5 is the result of the option being exercised. The investor has to buy the stock for $25 in September and sell it to the purchaser of the option for $20.

Problem 1.16.

An investor writes a December put option with a strike price of $30. The price of the option is $4. Under what circumstances does the investor make a gain?

The investor makes a gain if the price of the stock is above $26 at the time of exercise. (This ignores the time value of money.)

4

Problem 1.17.
The CME Group offers a futures contract on long-term Treasury bonds. Characterize the investors likely to use this contract.

Most investors will use the contract because they want to do one of the following:
   a) Hedge an exposure to long-term interest rates.
   b) Speculate on the future direction of long-term interest rates.
   c) Arbitrage between the spot and futures markets for Treasury bonds.
The contract is discussed in Chapter 6.

Problem 1.18.
An airline executive has argued: "There is no point in our using oil futures. There is just as much chance that the price of oil in the future will be less than the futures price as there is that it will be greater than this price." Discuss the executive's viewpoint.

It may well be true that there is just as much chance that the price of oil in the future will be above the futures price as that it will be below the futures price. This means that the use of a futures contract for speculation would be like betting on whether a coin comes up heads or tails. But it might make sense for the airline to use futures for hedging rather than speculation. The futures contract then has the effect of reducing risks. It can be argued that an airline should not expose its shareholders to risks associated with the future price of oil when there are contracts available to hedge the risks.

Problem 1.19.
"Options and futures are zero-sum games." What do you think is meant by this statement?

The statement means that the gain to one party always equals the loss the other party. The total gain to the two parties is always zero.

Problem 1.20.
A trader enters into a short forward contract on 100 million yen. The forward exchange rate is $0.0080 per yen. How much does the trader gain or lose if the exchange rate at the end of the contract is (a) $0.0074 per yen; (b) $0.0091 per yen?

   a) The trader sells 100 million yen for $0.0080 per yen when the exchange rate is $0.0074 per yen. The gain is 100×0.0006 millions of dollars or $60,000.
   b) The trader sells 100 million yen for $0.0080 per yen when the exchange rate is $0.0091 per yen. The loss is 100×0.0011 millions of dollars or $110,000.

Problem 1.21.
A trader enters into a short cotton futures contract when the futures price is 50 cents per pound. The contract is for the delivery of 50,000 pounds. How much does the trader gain or lose if the cotton price at the end of the contract is (a) 48.20 cents per pound; (b) 51.30 cents per pound?

   a) The trader sells for 50 cents per pound something that is worth 48.20 cents per pound. Gain =

($0.5000 − $0.4820) × 50,000 = $900.

b) The trader sells for 50 cents per pound something that is worth 51.30 cents per pound. Loss = ($0.5130 − $0.5000) × 50,000 = $650.

Problem 1.22.

A company knows that it is due to receive a certain amount of a foreign currency in four months. What type of option contract is appropriate for hedging?

A long position in a four-month put option can provide insurance against the exchange rate falling below the strike price. It ensures that the foreign currency can be sold for at least the strike price.

Problem 1.23.

A United States company expects to have to pay 1 million Canadian dollars in six months. Explain how the exchange rate risk can be hedged using (a) a forward contract; (b) an option.

The company could enter into a long forward contract to buy 1 million Canadian dollars in six months. This would have the effect of locking in an exchange rate equal to the current forward exchange rate. Alternatively the company could buy a call option giving it the right (but not the obligation) to purchase 1 million Canadian dollars at a certain exchange rate in six months. This would provide insurance against a strong Canadian dollar in six months while still allowing the company to benefit from a weak Canadian dollar at that time.

Problem 1.24

A trader buys a call option with a strike price of $30 for $3. Does the trader ever exercise the option and lose money on the trade. Explain.

Yes, the trader will exercise if the asset price is greater than $30, but will cover the cost of the call option only if the price is greater than $33. The trader exercises and loses money if the price is between $30 and $33.

Problem 1.25

A trader sells a put option with a strike price of $40 for $5. What is the trader's maximum gain and maximum loss? How does your answer change if it is a call option?

The trader's maximum gain from the put option is $5. The maximum loss is $35, corresponding to the situation where the option is exercised and the asset price is zero. If the option were a call, the trader's maximum gain would still be $5, but there would be no bound to the loss as there is in theory no limit to how high the asset price could rise.

Problem 1.26

"Buying a put option on the stock when the stock is owned is a form of insurance." Explain this statement.

If the stock price declines below the strike price of the put option, the stock can be sold for the strike price.

CHAPTER 2
Futures Markets and Central Counterparties

This chapter covers how futures markets work and how over-the-counter (OTC) derivatives are traded. Key things you should understand are (a) how futures contracts are entered into and closed out, (b) how the daily settlement procedures work for futures contracts, (c) the operation of margin accounts for futures contracts, and (d) the difference between bilateral and central clearing for OTC derivatives.

A long futures contract is an agreement to buy a certain amount of the underlying asset during a future month; a short futures contract is an agreement to sell a certain amount of the underlying asset during a future month. A trader can enter into a futures contract (long or short) by issuing appropriate instructions to a broker. Let's use the live cattle futures contracts in Table 2.2 as an example. Each contract is on 40,000 pounds of cattle. Suppose a trader shorts (i.e., sells) one December contract on May 13, 2015. (The High and Low columns in Table 2.2 indicate that the futures price at the time of this transaction is between 151.500 and 153.150 cents per pound.) The broker will ask the trader to provide "initial margin". Minimum levels for the initial margin for retail traders are specified by the exchange. The initial margin can be in the form of cash or marketable securities.

The settlement price on the contract is the price at which the contract trades at the close of trading on a day. It is 151.725 on May 12, 2015 for the live cattle contract we are considering. If the settlement price on December live cattle increases by 2 cents per pound from one day to the next, the trader we are considering loses $0.02 \times 40,000 = \$800$ from his or her margin account. (Because the trader has a short position, a futures price increase costs the trader money). Similarly, if the settlement price on December live cattle decreases by 2 cents per pound from one day to the next, $800 would be added to the trader's margin account. This procedure results in the futures contract being settled each day.

A maintenance margin (usually about 75% of the initial margin) is specified for retail traders. If the balance in the margin account falls below the maintenance margin level, the trader gets a margin call from the broker requiring that the balance in the margin account be brought up to the initial margin level. If the requested funds are not provided within 24 hours, the trader's position is closed out. A clearing house handles the flows of funds from the margin accounts of traders with short positions to the margin accounts of traders with long positions, or vice versa. Study the gold futures example in Table 2.1 and make sure you understand all the entries in the table.

The clearing house of the futures exchange has members who clear their own trades and those of brokers who are not themselves members. Members provide initial margin (lower than the initial margin required by brokers from retail investors). Unlike retail investors they are not subject to a maintenance margin. At the end of each day there is a cash settlement reflecting the gain or loss on the transactions for which they are responsible.

When a broker is instructed to close out a futures position (or when the broker closes a trader out because of a failure to meet a margin call), the broker does the opposite trade to the original one on the trader's behalf. For example, suppose the trader we have considered wanted to close out the short-one-contract December live cattle futures position on September 5, 2015. The trader's broker would contact the exchange to enter into a long December live cattle contract on trader's behalf. The long contract would cancel out the short contract and the trader would be left with no outstanding position. One of the attractions of futures contracts is that it is just as easy to take a long as a short position. Another is that it is just as easy to close out a position as to enter into it in the first place.

Most futures contracts are closed out prior to the delivery period, but a few do lead to delivery. It is the possibility of final delivery that ties the futures price to the spot price. When delivery takes place, it is the party with the short futures position that initiates delivery. The party with the short position may have some choices to make on exactly what is delivered, where it is delivered, and when it is delivered. Some contracts such as futures on stock indices are settled in cash rather than by physical delivery. In these cases, a single delivery date is specified for the contract. The contract is marked to market until this delivery date. On the delivery date, there is a final daily settlement, based on the spot value of the underlying asset, and all contracts are declared closed out.

One of the attractions of futures contracts for speculators is that they have built in leverage. The amount of cash provided to do a trade (the initial margin) is a relatively small percentage of the value of asset being traded (perhaps only 10%).

When you trade stocks there are many different types of orders that can be placed with a broker: market orders, limit orders, stop orders, stop-loss orders, and so on. As Section 2.8 indicates, the same types of orders can be placed in futures markets. The accounting and tax treatment of futures and other derivatives are complicated, but Section 2.10 provides an overview of the issues that are important in many jurisdictions. Normal accrual accounting leads to the profit or loss on a futures transaction being recognized throughout the life of the contract for both accounting and tax purposes. However, if a trader can show that a contract is entered into for hedging purposes, then the profit or loss on the contract is recognized when the contract is closed out (see Example 2.1.) The idea here is that for a hedger the cash flows from the futures contract should be matched with the cash flows from the underlying asset being hedged.

You should by now be fully comfortable with the differences between futures and forward contracts. These are summarized in Table 2.3. Both futures and forwards are agreements to buy or sell an asset at a future time for a specified price. Futures contracts are traded on an exchange; forward contracts are traded over-the counter. Futures contracts have standard terms defined by the exchange for the size of the contract, delivery dates, etc.; forward contracts are not standardized. Delivery in a futures contract can often take place on a number of different days during the delivery month; forward contracts normally have only one delivery date specified. Futures contracts are settled daily by the transfer of funds into or out of the margin account; forward contracts are settled at the end of the contract. Futures contracts are normally closed out prior to delivery; forward contracts are normally held to delivery. The margin and daily settlement in futures contracts have the effect of eliminating virtually all credit risk; there is some (small) credit risk in forward contracts.

As discussed in Section 2.5, over-the-counter derivatives markets are increasingly adopting practices similar to those of futures markets to reduce credit risk. Regulations introduced since the crisis are requiring standard OTC transactions between financial institutions to be cleared through central counterparties (CCPs). A CCP is very similar to an exchange clearing house. It has members who present trades for clearing. Members are required to post initial margin and there are daily variation margin flows between members reflecting the gains and losses on the transactions they are clearing.

Trades not cleared through a CCP are cleared bilaterally. This means that there is an agreement between the two companies covering how trades will be handled, whether collateral (i.e. margin) has to be provided, and so on. The difference between bilateral clearing and central clearing is summarized in Figure 2.2.

Answers to Practice Questions

Problem 2.8.
The party with a short position in a futures contract sometimes has options as to the precise asset that will be delivered, where delivery will take place, when delivery will take place, and so on. Do these options increase or decrease the futures price? Explain your reasoning.

These options make the contract less attractive to the party with the long position and more attractive to the party with the short position. They therefore tend to reduce the futures price.

Problem 2.9.
What are the most important aspects of the design of a new futures contract?

The most important aspects of the design of a new futures contract are the specification of the underlying asset, the size of the contract, the delivery arrangements, and the delivery months.

Problem 2.10.
Explain how margin protect futures traders against the possibility of default.

Margin is money deposited by a trader with his or her broker, by the broker with the clearing house member, and by the clearing house member with the clearing house. It acts as a guarantee that any losses on the futures contract will be covered. The balance in the margin account is adjusted daily to reflect gains and losses on the futures contract. If losses lead to the balance in thje margin account falling below a certain level (the maintenance margin), a trader is required to deposit further margin with the broker. This system makes it unlikely that the trader will default. A similar system of margin accounts makes it unlikely that the investor's broker will default on the contract it has with the clearing house member and unlikely that the clearing house member will default on its trades with the clearing house.

Problem 2.11.
A trader buys two July futures contracts on frozen orange juice. Each contract is for the delivery of 15,000 pounds. The current futures price is 120 cents per pound, the initial margin is $6,000 per contract, and the maintenance margin is $4,500 per contract. What price change would lead

to a margin call? Under what circumstances could $2,000 be withdrawn from the margin account?

There is a margin call if more than $1,500 is lost on one contract. This happens if the futures price of frozen orange juice falls by more than 10 cents to below 110 cents per lb. $2,000 can be withdrawn from the margin account if there is a gain on one contract of $1,000. This will happen if the futures price rises by 6.67 cents to 126.67 cents per lb.

Problem 2.12.
Show that, if the futures price of a commodity is greater than the spot price during the delivery period, then there is an arbitrage opportunity. Does an arbitrage opportunity exist if the futures price is less than the spot price? Explain your answer.

If the futures price is greater than the spot price during the delivery period, an arbitrageur buys the asset, shorts a futures contract, and makes delivery for an immediate profit. If the futures price is less than the spot price during the delivery period, there is no similar perfect arbitrage strategy. An arbitrageur can take a long futures position but cannot force immediate delivery of the asset. The decision on when delivery will be made is made by the party with the short position. Nevertheless companies interested in acquiring the asset will find it attractive to enter into a long futures contract and wait for delivery to be made.

Problem 2.13.
Explain the difference between a market-if-touched order and a stop order.

A market-if-touched order is executed at the best available price after a trade occurs at a specified price or at a price more favorable than the specified price. A stop order is executed at the best available price after there is a bid or offer at the specified price or at a price less favorable than the specified price.

Problem 2.14.
Explain what a stop-limit order to sell at 20.30 with a limit of 20.10 means.

A stop-limit order to sell at 20.30 with a limit of 20.10 means that as soon as there is a bid at 20.30 the contract should be sold providing this can be done at 20.10 or a higher price.

Problem 2.15.
At the end of one day a clearing house member is long 100 contracts, and the settlement price is $50,000 per contract. The original margin is $2,000 per contract. On the following day the member becomes responsible for clearing an additional 20 long contracts, entered into at a price of $51,000 per contract. The settlement price at the end of this day is $50,200. How much does the member have to add to its margin account with the exchange clearing house?

The clearing house member is required to provide $20 \times \$2,000 = \$40,000$ as initial margin for the new contracts. There is a gain of $(50,200 - 50,000) \times 100 = \$20,000$ on the existing contracts. There is also a loss of $(51,000 - 50,200) \times 20 = \$16,000$ on the new contracts. The member must therefore add

$$40{,}000 - 20{,}000 + 16{,}000 = \$36{,}000$$

to the margin account.

Problem 2.16.
Explain why collateral requirements will increase in the OTC markets as a result of new regulations introduced since the 2008 credit crisis.

Standard transactions between financial institutions have to be cleared through CCPs. Initial margin and variation margin are therefore required. Nonstandard transactions between financial institutions will continue to be cleared bilaterally, but the credit support annex (CSA) must include a requirement for initial margin from both sides as well as variation margin.

Problem 2.17.
The forward price on the Swiss franc for delivery in 45 days is quoted as 1.1000. The futures price for a contract that will be delivered in 45 days is 0.9000. Explain these two quotes. Which is more favorable for an investor wanting to sell Swiss francs?

The 1.1000 forward quote is the number of Swiss francs per dollar. The 0.9000 futures quote is the number of dollars per Swiss franc. When quoted in the same way as the futures price the forward price is $1/1.1000 = 0.9091$. The Swiss franc is therefore more valuable in the forward market than in the futures market. The forward market is therefore more attractive for an investor wanting to sell Swiss francs.

Problem 2.18.
Suppose you call your broker and issue instructions to sell one July hogs contract. Describe what happens.

Hog futures are traded by the CME Group. The broker will request some initial margin. The order will be relayed by telephone to your broker's trading desk on the floor of the exchange (or to the trading desk of another broker). It will be sent by messenger to a commission broker who will execute the trade according to your instructions. Confirmation of the trade eventually reaches you. If there are adverse movements in the futures price your broker may contact you to request additional margin.

Problem 2.19.
"Speculation in futures markets is pure gambling. It is not in the public interest to allow speculators to trade on a futures exchange." Discuss this viewpoint.

Speculators are important market participants because they add liquidity to the market. However, contracts must be useful for hedging as well as speculation. This is because regulators generally only approve contracts when they are likely to be of interest to hedgers as well as speculators.

Problem 2.20.
Explain the difference between bilateral and central clearing for OTC derivatives.

In bilateral clearing, two market participants enter into an agreement with each other covering all outstanding derivative transactions between the two parties. Typically the agreement covers collateral arrangements, events of default, the circumstances under which one side can terminate the transactions, etc. In central clearing, a CCP (central clearing party) stands between the two sides of an OTC derivative transaction in much the same way that the exchange clearing house does for exchange-traded contracts. The CCP and its members absorb the credit risk, but initial as well as variation margin is required from each side.

Problem 2.21.
What do you think would happen if an exchange started trading a contract in which the quality of the underlying asset was incompletely specified?

The contract would not be a success. Parties with short positions would hold their contracts until delivery and then deliver the cheapest form of the asset. This might well be viewed by the party with the long position as garbage! Once news of the quality problem became widely known no one would be prepared to buy the contract. This shows that futures contracts are feasible only when there are rigorous standards within an industry for defining the quality of the asset. Many futures contracts have in practice failed because of the problem of defining quality.

Problem 2.22.
"When a futures contract is traded on the floor of the exchange, it may be the case that the open interest increases by one, stays the same, or decreases by one." Explain this statement.

If both sides of the transaction are entering into a new contract, the open interest increases by one. If both sides of the transaction are closing out existing positions, the open interest decreases by one. If one party is entering into a new contract while the other party is closing out an existing position, the open interest stays the same.

Problem 2.23.
Suppose that on October 24, 2016, a company sells one April 2017 live-cattle futures contract. It closes out its position on January 21, 2017. The futures price (per pound) is 151.20 cents when it enters into the contract, 148.30 cents when it closes out the position and 148.80 cents at the end of December 2016. One contract is for the delivery of 40,000 pounds of cattle. What is the profit? How is it taxed if the company is (a) a hedger and (b) a speculator? Assume that the company has a December 31 year end.

The total profit is
$$40{,}000 \times (0.15120 - 0.14830) = \$1{,}160$$
If you are a hedger this is all taxed in 2017. If you are a speculator
$$40{,}000 \times (0.15120 - 0.14880) = \$960$$
is taxed in 2016 and
$$40{,}000 \times (0.14880 - 0.14830) = \$200$$
is taxed in 2017.

Problem 2.24
Explain how CCPs work. What are the advantages to the financial system of requiring all standardized derivatives transactions to be cleared through CCPs?

In fact it is only standard trades between financial institutions that must be cleared through CCPs. A CCP stands between the two parties in an OTC derivative transaction in much the same way that a clearing house does for exchange-traded contracts. The CCP and its members absorb the credit risk, but initial and variation margin is required from each side. In addition, CCP members are required to contribute to a default fund. The advantage to the financial system is that there is a lot more collateral (i.e., margin) available and it is therefore much less likely that a default by one major participant in the derivatives market will lead to losses by other market participants. There is also more transparency in that the trades of different market participants are more readily known. The disadvantage is that CCPs are replacing banks as the too-big-to-fail entities in the financial system. There clearly needs to be careful oversight of the management of CCPs.

CHAPTER 3
Hedging Strategies Using Futures

This chapter discusses how futures contracts can be used for hedging. If a company knows it will buy a certain asset at a certain future time, it can hedge its risk with a long futures position. The futures position is chosen so that (a) if the asset price increases, the gain on the futures position offsets the extra price that has to be paid for the asset and (b) if the asset price decreases the loss on the futures position is offset by the gain resulting from the lower price paid for the asset. Similarly, if a company knows it will sell a certain asset on a certain future date, it can hedge its risk with a short futures position. In this case, the futures position is chosen so that (a) if the asset price decreases the gain on the futures position offsets the loss on the amount realized for the asset and (b) if the asset price increases, the loss on the futures position is offset by the gain resulting from the higher price realized for the asset.

If you need to review statistical concepts such as standard deviation, correlation, and linear regression you should study the first three sections of the appendix to before reading Section 3.4. If you are unfamiliar with the capital asset pricing model, you should study the last section of the appendix before reading Section 3.5.

Hedging is designed to reduce risk. As such it should be attractive to corporations. The chapter discusses three reasons why corporations in practice often do not hedge. These reasons are

1. In some instances shareholders prefer companies not to hedge a risk. This might be because the shareholders want exposure to the risk. (For example, many shareholders buy the stock of particular gold mining companies because they want an exposure to the price of gold. They do not want those companies to hedge their gold price risk). It may also because shareholders can diversify away some of the risk within their own portfolios.
2. Sometimes a company may appear to have exposure to a particular market variable when a "big picture" view of its risks indicates little or no exposure. (See for example the gold jewelry manufacturer example in Table 3.1 or the farmer in Problem 3.17.)
3. Corporate treasurers are liable to be criticized if money is lost on the futures position and gained on the underlying position being hedged---even though this was part of the risk reduction strategy. The imaginary dialogue between a treasurer and a president at the end of Section 3.2 illustrates the problem. Note that we expect to lose money on about half of the futures contracts we enter into. The purpose of the futures contracts is to reduce risk not to increase expected profits.

An important concept is basis risk. This arises because a futures contract that is held for hedging purposes is almost always closed out prior to the delivery date. (As described in the chapter, the futures contract chosen normally has a delivery month later than the month when the underlying asset will be bought or sold.) The futures price on the close-out date does not equal the spot price. The basis is the spot price minus the futures price at this time. If you enter into a futures contract at time t_1 to hedge the purchase of an asset at time t_2 the price you effectively pay for the asset is the price at time t_2 adjusted for the gain/loss on the futures contract. This is the same as the futures price of the contract at time t_1 plus the basis at time t_2. Similarly, if you enter into a futures contract at time t_1 to hedge the sale of an asset at time t_2 the effective price you receive is the futures price at time t_1 plus the basis at time t_2. Examples illustrating this are Example 3.3 and Example 3.4. The futures price at time t_1 is known for certain when you initiate the hedge at time t_1. However, the basis at time t_2 is not known. The uncertainty associated with the price you pay or receive is therefore the uncertainty associated with the basis (which explains the term "basis risk").

The hedge ratio is the ratio of the size of the futures position to the size of the exposure being hedged. The normal situation is to use a hedge ratio of 1.0. The chapter describes two situations where a hedge ratio of 1.0 is not appropriate. One is when there is cross hedging; the other is when stock index futures are used. Cross hedging is not hedging done in anger! It involves a situation where the asset underlying the futures contract is different from the asset being hedged. In cross hedging the optimal hedge ratio is given by equation (3.1).

Stock index futures are often used by portfolio managers. They can be used to hedge a portfolio so that the manager is out of the market for a period of time. Alternatively they can be used to change the beta of a portfolio. A short futures position reduces the beta of the portfolio; a long futures position increases the beta of a portfolio. The number of contracts that should be traded is the desired change in beta multiplied by the ratio of the value of the portfolio to the value of the assets underlying one contract. Note that a full hedge (giving the portfolio manager no exposure to the market) corresponds to changing the beta of the portfolio to zero. You should study Table 3.4 to make sure you understand how the capital asset pricing model works and how futures contracts can eliminate market risk.

The final part of the chapter discusses what is known as "stack and roll." This is a way of creating a hedge that lasts a relatively long time from short-dated futures contracts. The way hedges are rolled forward is as follows. You enter into a short-dated futures contract, close it out just before the delivery month, immediately replace it with another short-dated futures contract, close it out just before the delivery month, and so on. (Metallgesellschaft in Business Snapshot 3.2 illustrates potential liquidity problems in a stack and roll strategy.) It is worth noting that hedges created in this way do not qualify for hedge accounting the United States.

Answers to Practice Questions

Problem 3.8.
In the CME Group's corn futures contract, the following delivery months are available: March, May, July, September, and December. State the contract that should be used for hedging when the expiration of the hedge is in
   a) June
   b) July
   c) January

A good rule of thumb is to choose a futures contract that has a delivery month as close as possible to, but later than, the month containing the expiration of the hedge. The contracts that should be used are therefore

(a) July

(b) September

(c) March

Problem 3.9.

Does a perfect hedge always succeed in locking in the current spot price of an asset for a future transaction? Explain your answer.

No. Consider, for example, the use of a forward contract to hedge a known cash inflow in a foreign currency. The forward contract locks in the forward exchange rate, which is in general different from the spot exchange rate.

Problem 3.10.

Explain why a short hedger's position improves when the basis strengthens unexpectedly and worsens when the basis weakens unexpectedly.

The basis is the amount by which the spot price exceeds the futures price. A short hedger is long the asset and short futures contracts. The value of his or her position therefore improves as the basis increases. Similarly it worsens as the basis decreases.

Problem 3.11.

Imagine you are the treasurer of a Japanese company exporting electronic equipment to the United States. Discuss how you would design a foreign exchange hedging strategy and the arguments you would use to sell the strategy to your fellow executives.

The simple answer to this question is that the treasurer should
  1. Estimate the company's future cash flows in Japanese yen and U.S. dollars
  2. Enter into forward and futures contracts to lock in the exchange rate for the U.S. dollar cash flows.

However, this is not the whole story. As the gold jewelry example in Table 3.1 shows, the company should examine whether the magnitudes of the foreign cash flows depend on the exchange rate. For example, will the company be able to raise the price of its product in U.S. dollars if the yen appreciates? If the company can do so, its foreign exchange exposure may be quite low. The key estimates required are those showing the overall effect on the company's profitability of changes in the exchange rate at various times in the future. Once these estimates have been produced the company can choose between using futures and options to hedge its risk. The results of the analysis should be presented carefully to other executives. It should be explained that a hedge does not ensure that profits will be higher. It means that profit will be more certain. When futures/forwards are used both the downside and upside are eliminated. With options a premium is paid to eliminate only the downside.

Problem 3.12.

Suppose that in Example 3.4 the company decides to use a hedge ratio of 0.8. How does the decision affect the way in which the hedge is implemented and the result?

If the hedge ratio is 0.8, the company takes a long position in 16 December oil futures contracts

on June 8 when the futures price is $8. It closes out its position on November 10. The spot price and futures price at this time are $65 and $62. The gain on the futures position is
$$(62 - 58) \times 16{,}000 = \$64{,}000$$
The effective cost of the oil is therefore
$$20{,}000 \times 65 - 64{,}000 = \$1{,}236{,}000$$
or $61.80 per barrel. (This compares with $61.00 per barrel when the company is fully hedged.)

Problem 3.13.
"If the minimum-variance hedge ratio is calculated as 1.0, the hedge must be perfect." Is this statement true? Explain your answer.

The statement is not true. The minimum variance hedge ratio is
$$\rho \frac{\sigma_S}{\sigma_F}$$
It is 1.0 when $\rho = 0.5$ and $\sigma_S = 2\sigma_F$. Since $\rho < 1.0$ the hedge is clearly not perfect.

Problem 3.14.
"If there is no basis risk, the minimum variance hedge ratio is always 1.0." Is this statement true? Explain your answer.

The statement is true. Suppose for the sake of definiteness that the commodity is being purchased. If the hedge ratio is h, the gain on futures is $h(F_2 - F_1)$ so that the price paid is
$S_2 - h(F_2 - F_1)$ or $hb_2 + hF_1 + (1-h)S_2$.
If there is no basis risk, b_2 is known. For a given h, there is therefore no uncertainty in the first two terms. For any value of h other than 1, there is uncertainty in the third term. The minimum variance hedge ratio is therefore 1.

Problem 3.15
"When the futures price of an asset is less than its spot price, long hedges are likely to be particularly attractive." Explain this statement.

A company that knows it will purchase a commodity in the future is able to lock in a price close to the futures price. This is likely to be particularly attractive when the futures price is less than the spot price. An illustration is provided by Example 3.2.

Problem 3.16.
The standard deviation of monthly changes in the spot price of live cattle is (in cents per pound) 1.2. The standard deviation of monthly changes in the futures price of live cattle for the closest contract is 1.4. The correlation between the futures price changes and the spot price changes is 0.7. It is now October 15. A beef producer is committed to purchasing 200,000 pounds of live cattle on November 15. The producer wants to use the December live-cattle futures contracts to hedge its risk. Each contract is for the delivery of 40,000 pounds of cattle. What strategy should the beef producer follow?

The optimal hedge ratio is

$$0.7 \times \frac{1.2}{1.4} = 0.6$$

The beef producer requires a long position in $200000 \times 0.6 = 120,000$ lbs of cattle. The beef producer should therefore take a long position in 3 December contracts closing out the position on November 15.

Problem 3.17.

A corn farmer argues "I do not use futures contracts for hedging. My real risk is not the price of corn. It is that my whole crop gets wiped out by the weather."Discuss this viewpoint. Should the farmer estimate his or her expected production of corn and hedge to try to lock in a price for expected production?

If weather creates a significant uncertainty about the volume of corn that will be harvested, the farmer should not enter into short forward contracts to hedge the price risk on his or her expected production. The reason is as follows. Suppose that the weather is bad and the farmer's production is lower than expected. Other farmers are likely to have been affected similarly. Corn production overall will be low and as a consequence the price of corn will be relatively high. The farmer's problems arising from the bad harvest will be made worse by losses on the short futures position. This problem emphasizes the importance of looking at the big picture when hedging. The farmer is correct to question whether hedging price risk while ignoring other risks is a good strategy.

Problem 3.18.

On July 1, an investor holds 50,000 shares of a certain stock. The market price is $30 per share. The investor is interested in hedging against movements in the market over the next month and decides to use the September Mini S&P 500 futures contract. The index is currently 1,500 and one contract is for delivery of $50 times the index. The beta of the stock is 1.3. What strategy should the investor follow?

A short position in

$$1.3 \times \frac{50,000 \times 30}{50 \times 1,500} = 26$$

contracts is required. It will be profitable if the stock outperforms the market in the sense that its return is greater than that predicted by the capital asset pricing model.

Problem 3.19.

Suppose that in Table 3.5 the company decides to use a hedge ratio of 1.5. How does the decision affect the way the hedge is implemented and the result?

If the company uses a hedge ratio of 1.5 in Table 3.5, it would at each stage short 150 contracts. The gain from the futures contracts would be

$$1.50 \times 1.70 = \$2.55$$

per barrel and the company would be $0.85 per barrel better off than with a hedge ratio of one.

Problem 3.20.

A futures contract is used for hedging. Explain why the daily settlement of the contract can give

18

rise to cash flow problems.

Suppose that you enter into a short futures contract to hedge the sale of an asset in six months. If the price of the asset rises sharply during the six months, the futures price will also rise and you may get margin calls. The margin calls will lead to cash outflows. Eventually the cash outflows will be offset by the extra amount you get when you sell the asset, but there is a mismatch in the timing of the cash outflows and inflows. Your cash outflows occur earlier than your cash inflows. A similar situation could arise if you used a long position in a futures contract to hedge the purchase of an asset and the asset's price fell sharply. An extreme example of what we are talking about here is provided by Metallgesellschaft (see Business Snapshot 3.2).

Problem 3.21.
The expected return on the S&P 500 is 12% and the risk-free rate is 5%. What is the expected return on the investment with a beta of (a) 0.2, (b) 0.5, and (c) 1.4?

a) $0.05+0.2\times(0.12-0.05) = 0.064$ or 6.4%
b) $0.05+0.5\times(0.12-0.05) = 0.085$ or 8.5%
c) $0.05+1.4\times(0.12-0.05) = 0.148$ or 14.8%

CHAPTER 4
Interest Rates

This chapter provides background material on interest rates. Understanding this material is essential for the rest of the book. The chapter starts by discussing several interest rates that are important to derivatives markets: Treasury rates, LIBOR rates, overnight rates, and repo rates. It also provides a brief description of swaps where LIBOR is swapped for a fixed rate and overnight rates are swapped for a fixed rate. (Swaps are discussed more fully in Chapter 7.)

The concept of a "risk-free rate" is important in derivatives pricing. In the past traders have used LIBOR rates as proxies for risk-free rates. Derivatives market participants now use another rate, the overnight indexed swap rate, as a proxy for the risk-free rate. That is why it is introduced in this chapter.

It is important that you understand the compounding frequency material in Section 4.4. It cannot be emphasized enough that the compounding frequency is nothing more than a unit of measurement. Consider two interest rates. One is 10% with semiannual compounding; the other is 10.25% with annual compounding. The interest rates are the same. They are just measured in different units. Converting an interest rate from one compounding frequency to another is like converting a distance from miles to kilometers. The concept of a continuously compounded interest rate is likely to be new to many readers. As we increase the compounding frequency when measuring interest rates, in the limit we get a unit of measurement known as continuous compounding. The formulas in options markets involve rates measured with continuous compounding and, except where otherwise stated, the rates in the book are measured with continuous compounding. It is therefore important that you make sure you become comfortable with continuously compounded rates. Equations (4.3) and (4.4) show how to convert a rate from a compounding frequency of m times per year to continuous compounding and vice versa. The appendix to the chapter provides a review of exponential and logarithmic functions for readers who are not familiar with these functions.

The rates that are quoted in financial markets are often the rates corresponding to a situation where interest payments are made regularly (e.g., every six months). The rates important in derivatives markets are zero-coupon rates (sometimes referred to as zero rates). These are the rates that correspond to a situation where money is invested at time 0 and all the return (interest and principal) is realized at some future time T. Plotting the zero rate as a function of the maturity T gives the zero-coupon term structure of interest rates. The discount rate that should be used for a cash flow occurring at time T is a zero-coupon interest rate for maturity T.

Two definitions should be noted. A bond yield is the discount rate for the cash flows on a bond that causes the bond price to equal the market price. (For this purpose, the discount rate is assumed to be the same for each cash flow) The par yield for a bond is the coupon rate that causes the bond price to equal its par value.

Section 4.7 describes a procedure for calculating zero rates known as the bootstrap method. First a short-term interest rate is determined from the shortest maturity instrument. Successively longer maturity instruments are then considered and used to calculate successively longer maturity rates. The method is used to determine zero rates from the prices of Treasury instruments and zero rates from overnight indexed swap rates.

Forward rates are the future rates of interest implied by zero-coupon interest rates. For example, if the one-year rate is 6% and the two-year rate is 8%, the forward rate for the second year is 10%. This is because 10% for the second year combined with 6% for the first year gives 8% for the two years. Note that this calculation is exact if the interest rates are measured with continuous compounding and only approximate when other compounding frequencies are used. A forward rate agreement (FRA) is an agreement that a certain interest rate will apply to a certain principal for a certain future time period. If the interest rate in the FRA is the forward rate, the value of the FRA is zero. Otherwise the value must be calculated using equations (4.9) and (4.10).

The chapter concludes by discussing the determinants of the term structure of interest rates. If market participants expect interest rates to rise in the future, the term structure will tend to be upward sloping and if market participants expect interest rates to fall it will tend to be downward sloping. However, as Section 4.10 points out, this is not the whole story. There is a natural tendency for people to want to borrow for long periods of time and lend for short periods of time. In order to encourage more people to borrow for short periods and invest their money for long periods banks tend to raise the long-term interest rates they offer relative to the expectations of market participants.

Software

In DG400f.xls, the Zero_Curve worksheet allows you to calculateeither a Treasury zero curve or an OIS zero curve from quotes. The Bond_Price worksheet allows you to value bonds. In both cases, the data displayed when you first open the worksheets correspond to the examples in the book.

Answers to Practice Questions

Problem 4.8.
The cash prices of six-month and one-year Treasury bills are 94.0 and 89.0. A 1.5-year bond that will pay coupons of $4 every six months currently sells for $94.84. A two-year bond that will pay coupons of $5 every six months currently sells for $97.12. Calculate the six-month, one-year, 1.5-year, and two-year zero rates.

The 6-month Treasury bill provides a return of $6/94 = 6.383\%$ in six months. This is $2 \times 6.383 = 12.766\%$ per annum with semiannual compounding or $2\ln(1.06383) = 12.38\%$ per annum with continuous compounding. The 12-month rate is $11/89 = 12.360\%$ with annual compounding or $\ln(1.1236) = 11.65\%$ with continuous compounding.

For the $1\frac{1}{2}$ year bond we must have

$$4e^{-0.1238 \times 0.5} + 4e^{-0.1165 \times 1} + 104e^{-1.5R} = 94.84$$

where R is the $1\frac{1}{2}$ year zero rate. It follows that

$$3.76 + 3.56 + 104e^{-1.5R} = 94.84$$
$$e^{-1.5R} = 0.8415$$
$$R = 0.115$$

or 11.5%. For the 2-year bond we must have
$$5e^{-0.1238 \times 0.5} + 5e^{-0.1165 \times 1} + 5e^{-0.115 \times 1.5} + 105e^{-2R} = 97.12$$
where R is the 2-year zero rate. It follows that
$$e^{-2R} = 0.7977$$
$$R = 0.113$$

or 11.3%.

Problem 4.9.

What rate of interest with continuous compounding is equivalent to 15% per annum with monthly compounding?

The rate of interest is R where:

$$e^{R} = \left(1 + \frac{0.15}{12}\right)^{12}$$

i.e.,

$$R = 12 \ln\left(1 + \frac{0.15}{12}\right)$$

$$= 0.1491$$

The rate of interest is therefore 14.91% per annum.

Problem 4.10.

A deposit account pays 12% per annum with continuous compounding, but interest is actually paid quarterly. How much interest will be paid each quarter on a $10,000 deposit?

The equivalent rate of interest with quarterly compounding is R where

$$e^{0.12} = \left(1 + \frac{R}{4}\right)^{4}$$

or

$$R = 4(e^{0.03} - 1) = 0.1218$$

The amount of interest paid each quarter is therefore:

$$10,000 \times \frac{0.1218}{4} = 304.55$$

or $304.55.

Problem 4.11.

Suppose that 6-month, 12-month, 18-month, 24-month, and 30-month zero rates are 4%, 4.2%, 4.4%, 4.6%, and 4.8% per annum with continuous compounding respectively. Estimate the cash price of a bond with a face value of 100 that will mature in 30 months and pays a coupon of 4% per annum semiannually.

The bond pays $2 in 6, 12, 18, and 24 months, and $102 in 30 months. The cash price is
$$2e^{-0.04\times0.5} + 2e^{-0.042\times1.0} + 2e^{-0.044\times1.5} + 2e^{-0.046\times2} + 102e^{-0.048\times2.5} = 98.04$$

Problem 4.12.
A three-year bond provides a coupon of 8% semiannually and has a cash price of 104. What is the bond's yield?

The bond pays $4 in 6, 12, 18, 24, and 30 months, and $104 in 36 months. The bond yield is the value of y that solves
$$4e^{-0.5y} + 4e^{-1.0y} + 4e^{-1.5y} + 4e^{-2.0y} + 4e^{-2.5y} + 104e^{-3.0y} = 104$$
Using the *Goal Seek* or *Solver* tool in Excel $y = 0.06407$ or 6.407%.

Problem 4.13.
Suppose that the 6-month, 12-month, 18-month, and 24-month zero rates are 5%, 6%, 6.5%, and 7% respectively. What is the two-year par yield?

Using the notation in the text, $m = 2$, $d = e^{-0.07\times2} = 0.8694$. Also
$$A = e^{-0.05\times0.5} + e^{-0.06\times1.0} + e^{-0.065\times1.5} + e^{-0.07\times2.0} = 3.6935$$
The formula in the text gives the par yield as
$$\frac{(100 - 100\times0.8694)\times2}{3.6935} = 7.0741$$
To verify that this is correct we calculate the value of a bond that pays a coupon of 7.0741% per year (that is 3.5370 every six months). The value is
$$3.537e^{-0.05\times0.5} + 3.537e^{-0.06\times1.0} + 3.537e^{-0.065\times1.5} + 103.537e^{-0.07\times2.0} = 100$$

verifying that 7.0741% is the par yield.

Problem 4.14.
Suppose that risk-free zero interest rates with continuous compounding are as follows:

Maturity(years)	Rate (% per annum)
1	2.0
2	3.0
3	3.7
4	4.2
5	4.5

Calculate forward interest rates for the second, third, fourth, and fifth years.

The forward rates with continuous compounding are as follows: to
Year 2: 4.0%
Year 3: 5.1%

Year 4: 5.7%
Year 5: 5.7%

Problem 4.15.

Use the risk-free rates in Problem 4.14 to value an FRA where you will pay 5% for the third year and receive LIBOR on $1 million. The forward LIBOR rate (annually compounded) for the third year is 5.5%.

The 3-year risk-free interest rate is 3.7% with continuous compounding. From equation (4.10), the value of the FRA is therefore

$$[1,000,000 \times (0.055 - 0.05) \times 1]e^{-0.037 \times 3} = 4,474.69$$

or $4,474.69.

Problem 4.16.

A 10-year, 8% Treasury coupon bond currently sells for $90. A 10-year, 4% coupon Treasury bond currently sells for $80. What is the 10-year zero rate? (Hint: Consider taking a long position in two of the 4% coupon bonds and a short position in one of the 8% coupon bonds.)

Taking a long position in two of the 4% coupon bonds and a short position in one of the 8% coupon bonds leads to the following cash flows

$$\text{Year 0:} \quad 90 - 2 \times 80 = -70$$
$$\text{Year 10:} \quad 200 - 100 = 100$$

because the coupons cancel out. $100 in 10 years time is equivalent to $70 today. The 10-year rate, R, (continuously compounded) is therefore given by

$$100 = 70e^{10R}$$

The rate is

$$\frac{1}{10} \ln \frac{100}{70} = 0.0357$$

or 3.57% per annum.

Problem 4.17.

Explain carefully why liquidity preference theory is consistent with the observation that the term structure of interest rates tends to be upward sloping more often than it is downward sloping.

If long-term rates were simply a reflection of expected future short-term rates, we would expect the term structure to be downward sloping as often as it is upward sloping. (This is based on the assumption that half of the time investors expect rates to increase and half of the time investors expect rates to decrease). Liquidity preference theory argues that long term rates are high relative to expected future short-term rates. This means that the term structure should be upward sloping more often than it is downward sloping.

Problem 4.18.

"When the zero curve is upward sloping, the zero rate for a particular maturity is greater than the par yield for that maturity. When the zero curve is downward sloping the reverse is true." Explain why this is so.

The par yield is the yield on a coupon-bearing bond. The zero rate is the yield on a zero-coupon bond. When the yield curve is upward sloping, the yield on an N-year coupon-bearing bond is less than the yield on an N-year zero-coupon bond. This is because the coupons are discounted at a lower rate than the N-year rate and drag the yield down below this rate. Similarly, when the yield curve is downward sloping, the yield on an N-year coupon bearing bond is higher than the yield on an N-year zero-coupon bond.

Problem 4.19.
Why are U.S. Treasury rates significantly lower than other rates that are close to risk free?

Two reasons (see Section 4.3) are:
1. A bank is required to hold no capital to support an investment in Treasury bills and bonds, but capital is required to support a similar investment in other very-low-risk instruments.
2. In the United States, Treasury instruments are given a favorable tax treatment compared with most other fixed-income investments because they are not taxed at the state level.

Problem 4.20.
Why does a loan in the repo market involve very little credit risk?

A repo is a contract where an investment dealer who owns securities agrees to sell them to another company now and buy them back later at a slightly higher price. The other company is providing a loan to the investment dealer. This loan involves very little credit risk. If the borrower does not honor the agreement, the lending company simply keeps the securities. If the lending company does not keep to its side of the agreement, the original owner of the securities keeps the cash.

Problem 4.21.
Explain why an FRA is equivalent to the exchange of a floating rate of interest for a fixed rate of interest?

A FRA is an agreement that a certain specified interest rate, R_K, will apply to a certain principal, L, for a certain specified future time period. Suppose that the floating rate observed in the market for the future time period at the beginning of the time period proves to be R_M. The FRA can be viewed as an exchange of interest at rate R_K for interest at rate R_M on a principal of L.

Problem 4.22.
Explain how a repo agreement works and why it involves very little risk for the lender.

The borrower transfers to the lender ownership of securities which have a value approximately equal to the amount borrowed and agrees to buy them back for the amount borrowed plus accrued interest at the end of the life of the loan. If the borrower defaults, the lender keeps the securities. Note that the securities should not have a value significantly more or less than the amount borrowed. Otherwise the risk of a loss if the borrower does not repay or the lender does sell the securities back as agreed may be unacceptable.

CHAPTER 5
Determination of Forward and Futures Prices

This chapter explores the relationship between forward/futures prices and spot prices. An important distinction is between investment and consumption assets. Investment assets are assets held solely for investment by at least some traders (but not necessarily all traders). Consumption assets are assets that are held primarily for consumption.

Investment assets can be divided into three categories:

1. Those that provide no income. (A Treasury bill falls into this category.)
2. Those that provide a known cash income. (A Treasury bond falls into this category.)
3. Those that provide a known yield (i.e. the income as a percentage of the asset price is known). Stock indices are usually assumed to provide a known yield.

For investment assets in the first category, the relationship between the forward price and the spot price is given by equation (5.1); for those in the second category, it is given by equation (5.2); for those in the third category, it is given by equation (5.3). The relationships can be proved by no arbitrage arguments. If a forward price is higher than that the price given by equations (5.1) to (5.3), market participants will lock in a profit by shorting the forward contract and buying the asset. If the forward price is lower than this price, market participants will lock in a profit by doing the reverse: taking a long position in the forward contract and selling (or shorting) the asset.

The difference between the forward price of an asset and the value of a forward contract often causes confusion. The forward price of an asset for a particular maturity date is the delivery price that would be negotiated today for a forward contract with that maturity date. The value of a forward contract with a certain maturity date and a certain delivery price is the contract's economic value. When a forward contract is first entered into, the value of the forward contract is zero and the delivery price is set equal to the forward price. As time goes by, the forward price changes but the delivery price of the contract remains the same. The value of the contract is liable to become positive or negative. Equation (5.4) gives the value of a long forward contract in terms of the forward price. If you are still unclear about the difference between the forward price and the value of the forward contract, try Problem 5.9.

Futures prices are more difficult to determine than forward prices because of the daily settlement in futures contracts. However, it turns out that in most situations the futures price for a contract with a certain maturity can be assumed to be the same as the forward price of a contract with that maturity. (The Eurodollar futures contract discussed in Chapter 6 provides an exception.) This means that equations (5.1) to (5.3) apply. A stock index is treated as an asset providing a yield equal to the dividend yield on the index. Equation (5.3) therefore applies with q equal to the average dividend yield on the index. A foreign currency is treated as an asset providing a yield equal to the foreign risk-free rate. It follows that in this instance equation (5.3) applies with q equal to the foreign risk-free rate (see equation 5.9).

For consumption assets there is no exact relationship between futures prices and spot prices. The relationship that exists for investment assets provides an upper bound for consumption assets. If the futures price is above this upper bound an arbitrageur can short futures and buy the asset to lock in a profit. However, if the futures price is below the upper bound there is no arbitrage opportunity. This is because the asset is not held for investment purposes. As a result, individuals who own the asset may not be prepared to forego the opportunity to consume the asset by selling it and buying the futures contract. For consumption assets an important concept is the convenience yield. This is a measure of the amount by which the futures price is less than its upper bound (see equation 5.17).

The last part of the chapter discusses the relationship between futures prices and expected future spot prices. If the asset has no systematic risk, the futures price equals the expected future spot price. If the asset has positive systematic risk, the futures price understates the expected future spot price. If the underlying asset has negative systematic risk, the futures price overstates the expected future spot price.

Answers to Practice Questions

Problem 5.8.
Is the futures price of a stock index greater than or less than the expected future value of the index? Explain your answer.

The futures price of a stock index is always less than the expected future value of the index. This follows from Section 5.14 and the fact that the index has positive systematic risk. For an alternative argument, let μ be the expected return required by investors on the index so that

$E(S_T) = S_0 e^{(\mu-q)T}$. Because $\mu > r$ and $F_0 = S_0 e^{(r-q)T}$, it follows that $E(S_T) > F_0$.

Problem 5.9.
A one-year long forward contract on a non-dividend-paying stock is entered into when the stock price is $40 and the risk-free rate of interest is 10% per annum with continuous compounding.

a) *What are the forward price and the initial value of the forward contract?*
b) *Six months later, the price of the stock is $45 and the risk-free interest rate is still 10%. What are the forward price and the value of the forward contract?*

a) The forward price, F_0, is given by equation (5.1) as:
$$F_0 = 40e^{0.1\times1} = 44.21$$
or $44.21. The initial value of the forward contract is zero.

b) The delivery price K in the contract is $44.21. The value of the contract, f, after six months is given by equation (5.5) as:
$$f = 45 - 44.21e^{-0.1\times0.5}$$

$$= 2.95$$
i.e., it is $2.95. The forward price is:

$$45e^{0.1\times0.5} = 47.31$$

or $47.31.

Problem 5.10.

The risk-free rate of interest is 7% per annum with continuous compounding, and the dividend yield on a stock index is 3.2% per annum. The current value of the index is 150. What is the six-month futures price?

Using equation (5.3) the six month futures price is
$$150e^{(0.07-0.032)\times0.5} = 152.88$$
or $152.88.

Problem 5.11.

Assume that the risk-free interest rate is 9% per annum with continuous compounding and that the dividend yield on a stock index varies throughout the year. In February, May, August, and November, dividends are paid at a rate of 5% per annum. In other months, dividends are paid at a rate of 2% per annum. Suppose that the value of the index on July 31 is 1,300. What is the futures price for a contract deliverable on December 31 of the same year?

The futures contract lasts for five months. The dividend yield is 2% for three of the months and 5% for two of the months. The average dividend yield is therefore
$$\frac{1}{5}(3\times2+2\times5) = 3.2\%$$

The futures price is therefore
$$1,300e^{(0.09-0.032)\times0.4167} = 1,331.80$$

or $1,331.80.

Problem 5.12.

Suppose that the risk-free interest rate is 10% per annum with continuous compounding and that the dividend yield on a stock index is 4% per annum. The index is standing at 400, and the futures price for a contract deliverable in four months is 405. What arbitrage opportunities does this create?

The theoretical futures price is
$$400e^{(0.10-0.04)\times4/12} = 408.08$$
The actual futures price is only 405. This shows that the index futures price is too low relative to the index. The correct arbitrage strategy is
  a) Buy futures contracts
  b) Short the shares underlying the index.

Problem 5.13.

Estimate the difference between short-term interest rates in Japan and the United States on May 13, 2015 from the information in Table 5.4.

The settlement prices for the futures contracts are to

Sept: 0.8345
Dec: 0.8355
The December 2015 price is about 0.12% above the September 2015 price. This suggests that the short-term interest rate in the United States exceeded short-term interest rate in Japan by about 0.12% per three months or about 0.48% per year.

Problem 5.14.
The two-month interest rates in Switzerland and the United States are 1% and 2% per annum, respectively, with continuous compounding. The spot price of the Swiss franc is $1.0600. The futures price for a contract deliverable in two months is $1.0500. What arbitrage opportunities does this create?

The theoretical futures price is
$$1.0600e^{(0.02-0.01)\times 2/12} = 1.0618$$

The actual futures price is too low. This suggests that an arbitrageur should sell Swiss francs and buy Swiss francs futures.

Problem 5.15.
The current price of silver is $30 per ounce. The storage costs are $0.48 per ounce per year payable quarterly in advance. Assuming that interest rates are 10% per annum for all maturities, calculate the futures price of silver for delivery in nine months.

The present value of the storage costs for nine months are
$$0.12 + 0.12e^{-0.10\times 0.25} + 0.12e^{-0.10\times 0.5} = 0.351$$
or $0.351. The futures price is from equation (5.11) given by F_0 where
$$F_0 = (30 + 0.351)e^{0.1\times 0.75} = 32.72$$

i.e., it is $32.72 per ounce.

Problem 5.16.
Suppose that F_1 and F_2 are two futures prices on the same commodity where the times to maturity of the contracts are t_1 and t_2 with $t_2 > t_1$. Prove that
$$F_2 \le F_1 e^{r(t_2-t_1)}$$
where r is the interest rate (assumed constant) and there are no storage costs. For the purposes of this problem, assume that a futures contract is the same as a forward contract.

If
$$F_2 > F_1 e^{r(t_2-t_1)}$$
an investor could make a riskless profit by
    a) taking a long position in a futures contract which matures at time t_1; and
    b) taking a short position in a futures contract which matures at time t_2
When the first futures contract matures, the asset is purchased for F_1 using funds borrowed at rate r. It is then held until time t_2 at which point it is exchanged for F_2 under the second contract. The

costs of the funds borrowed and accumulated interest at time t_2 is $F_1 e^{r(t_2-t_1)}$. A positive profit of

$$F_2 - F_1 e^{r(t_2-t_1)}$$

is then realized at time t_2. This type of arbitrage opportunity cannot exist for long. Hence:

$$F_2 \leq F_1 e^{r(t_2-t_1)}$$

Problem 5.17.

When a known future cash outflow in a foreign currency is hedged by a company using a forward contract, there is no foreign exchange risk. When it is hedged using futures contracts, the daily settlement process does leave the company exposed to some risk. Explain the nature of this risk. In particular, consider whether the company is better off using a futures contract or a forward contract when

    a) *The value of the foreign currency falls rapidly during the life of the contract*
    b) *The value of the foreign currency rises rapidly during the life of the contract*
    c) *The value of the foreign currency first rises and then falls back to its initial value*
    d) *The value of the foreign currency first falls and then rises back to its initial value*

Assume that the forward price equals the futures price.

In total the gain or loss under a futures contract is equal to the gain or loss under the corresponding forward contract. However the timing of the cash flows is different. When the time value of money is taken into account a futures contract may prove to be more valuable or less valuable than a forward contract. Of course the company does not know in advance which will work out better. The long forward contract provides a perfect hedge. The long futures contract provides a slightly imperfect hedge.

a) In this case, the forward contract would lead to a slightly better outcome. The company will make a loss on its hedge. If the hedge is with a forward contract, the whole of the loss will be realized at the end. If it is with a futures contract, the loss will be realized day by day throughout the contract. On a present value basis the former is preferable.

b) In this case, the futures contract would lead to a slightly better outcome. The company will make a gain on the hedge. If the hedge is with a forward contract, the gain will be realized at the end. If it is with a futures contract, the gain will be realized day by day throughout the life of the contract. On a present value basis the latter is preferable.

c) In this case, the futures contract would lead to a slightly better outcome. This is because it would involve positive cash flows early and negative cash flows later.

d) In this case, the forward contract would lead to a slightly better outcome. This is because, in the case of the futures contract, the early cash flows would be negative and the later cash flow would be positive.

Problem 5.18.

It is sometimes argued that a forward exchange rate is an unbiased predictor of future exchange rates. Under what circumstances is this so?

From the discussion in Section 5.14 of the text, the forward exchange rate is an unbiased predictor of the future exchange rate when the exchange rate has no systematic risk. To have no systematic risk the exchange rate must be uncorrelated with the return on the market.

Problem 5.19.
Show that the growth rate in an index futures price equals the excess return of the portfolio underlying the index over the risk-free rate. Assume that the risk-free interest rate and the dividend yield are constant.

Suppose that F_0 is the futures price at time zero for a contract maturing at time T and F_1 is the futures price for the same contract at time t_1. It follows that

$$F_0 = S_0 e^{(r-q)T}$$

$$F_1 = S_1 e^{(r-q)(T-t_1)}$$

where S_0 and S_1 are the spot price at times zero and t_1, r is the risk-free rate, and q is the dividend yield. These equations imply that

$$\frac{F_1}{F_0} = \frac{S_1}{S_0} e^{-(r-q)t_1}$$

Define the excess return of the portfolio underlying the index over the risk-free rate as x. The total return is $r + x$ and the return realized in the form of capital gains is $r + x - q$. It follows that $S_1 = S_0 e^{(r+x-q)t_1}$ and the above equation for reduces to

$$\frac{F_1}{F_0} = e^{xt_1}$$

which is the required result.

Problem 5.20.
Show that equation (5.3) is true by considering an investment in the asset combined with a short position in a futures contract. Assume that all income from the asset is reinvested in the asset. Use an argument similar to that in footnotes 2 and 4 and explain in detail what an arbitrageur would do if equation (5.3) did not hold.

Suppose we buy N units of the asset and invest the income from the asset in the asset. The income from the asset causes our holding in the asset to grow at a continuously compounded rate q. By time T our holding has grown to Ne^{qT} units of the asset. Analogously to footnotes 2 and 4 of Chapter 5, we therefore buy N units of the asset at time zero at a cost of S_0 per unit and enter into a forward contract to sell Ne^{qT} units for F_0 per unit at time T. This generates the following cash flows:

Time 0: $\qquad -NS_0$

Time 1: $\qquad NF_0 e^{qT}$

Because there is no uncertainty about these cash flows, the present value of the time T inflow must equal the time zero outflow when we discount at the risk-free rate. This means that

$$NS_0 = (NF_0 e^{qT})e^{-rT}$$

or

$$F_0 = S_0 e^{(r-q)T}$$

This is equation (5.3).

If $F_0 > S_0 e^{(r-q)T}$, an arbitrageur should borrow money at rate r and buy N units of the asset. At the same time the arbitrageur should enter into a forward contract to sell Ne^{qT} units of the asset at time T. As income is received, it is reinvested in the asset. At time T the loan is repaid and the arbitrageur makes a profit of $N(F_0 e^{qT} - S_0 e^{rT})$ at time T.

If $F_0 < S_0 e^{(r-q)T}$, an arbitrageur should short N units of the asset investing the proceeds at rate r. At the same time the arbitrageur should enter into a forward contract to buy Ne^{qT} units of the asset at time T. When income is paid on the asset, the arbitrageur owes money on the short position. The investor meets this obligation from the cash proceeds of shorting further units. The result is that the number of units shorted grows at rate q to Ne^{qT}. The cumulative short position is closed out at time T and the arbitrageur makes a profit of $N(S_0 e^{rT} - F_0 e^{qT})$.

Problem 5.21.
Explain carefully what is meant by the expected price of a commodity on a particular future date. Suppose that the futures price of crude oil declines with the maturity of the contract at the rate of 2% per year. Assume that speculators tend to be short crude oil futures and hedgers tended to be long crude oil futures. What does the Keynes and Hicks argument imply about the expected future price of oil?

To understand the meaning of the expected future price of a commodity, suppose that there are N different possible prices at a particular future time: P_1, P_2, ..., P_N. Define q_i as the (subjective) probability the price being P_i (with $q_1 + q_2 + ... + q_N = 1$). The expected future price is

$$\sum_{i=1}^{N} q_i P_i$$

Different people may have different expected future prices for the commodity. The expected future price in the market can be thought of as some sort of average of the opinions of different market participants. Of course, in practice the actual price of the commodity at the future time may prove to be higher or lower than the expected price.

Keynes and Hicks argue that speculators on average make money from commodity futures trading and hedgers on average lose money from commodity futures trading. If speculators tend to have short positions in crude oil futures, the Keynes and Hicks argument implies that futures prices overstate expected future spot prices. If crude oil futures prices decline at 2% per year the Keynes and Hicks argument therefore implies an even faster decline for the expected price of crude oil if speculators are short.

Problem 5.22.
The Value Line Index is designed to reflect changes in the value of a portfolio of over 1,600 equally weighted stocks. Prior to March 9, 1988, the change in the index from one day to the next was calculated as the geometric average of the changes in the prices of the stocks underlying the index. In these circumstances, does equation (5.8) correctly relate the futures

price of the index to its cash price? If not, does the equation overstate or understate the futures price?

When the geometric average of the price relatives is used, the changes in the value of the index do not correspond to changes in the value of a portfolio that is traded. Equation (5.8) is therefore no longer correct. The changes in the value of the portfolio are monitored by an index calculated from the arithmetic average of the prices of the stocks in the portfolio. Since the geometric average of a set of numbers is always less than the arithmetic average, equation (5.8) overstates the futures price. It is rumored that at one time (prior to 1988), equation (5.8) did hold for the Value Line Index. A major Wall Street firm was the first to recognize that this represented a trading opportunity. It made a financial killing by buying the stocks underlying the index and shorting the futures.

Problem 5.23.
What is meant by (a) an investment asset and (b) a consumption asset. Why is the distinction between investment and consumption assets important in the determination of forward and futures prices?

An investment asset is an asset held for investment by a non-neglible number of people or companies. A consumption asset is an asset that is nearly always held to be consumed (either directly or in some sort of manufacturing process). The forward/futures price can be determined from the spot price for an investment asset. In the case of a consumption asset all that can be determined is an upper bound for the forward/futures price.

Problem 5.24.
What is the cost of carry for (a) a non-dividend-paying stock, (b) a stock index, (c) a commodity with storage costs, and (d) a foreign currency?

a) the risk-free rate, b) the excess of the risk-free rate over the dividend yield c) the risk-free rate plus the storage cost, d) the excess of the domestic risk-free rate over the foreign risk-free rate.

CHAPTER 6
Interest Rate Futures

This chapter discusses how interest rate futures work and how they are used for hedging. To understand the way interest rate futures are quoted, it is necessary to understand day count conventions. The day count convention defines the number of days that the interest rate applies to and the way in which the interest earned accrues through time. Actual/actual in period, 30/360, and Actual/360 are popular day count conventions in the United States. Look at Business Snapshot 6.1 and Problem 6.19 to check that you understand how Actual/Actual in period (which applies to Treasury bonds) and 30/360 (which applies to corporate bonds) work.

Treasury bond futures contracts in the United States have some interesting delivery arrangements. For example, in the Treasury bond futures contract, any Treasury bond with a maturity between 15 and 25 years can be delivered. In the case of the Treasury note futures contract, any Treasury bond with a maturity of between 6.5 and 10 years can be delivered. (The party with the short position chooses which bond will be delivered and when during the delivery month it will be delivered.) To calculate how much is paid and received for the bond, the most recent futures prices is multiplied by a conversion factor and there is then an adjustment for accruals. Roughly speaking, the conversion factor is the price the bond would have if the zero-coupon yield curve were flat at 6% (semiannually compounded). Traders when they hold short futures positions and want to make delivery typically look at all the different bonds that can be delivered and calculate a cheapest-to-deliver bond.

The most important short-term futures contract in the United States is the three-month Eurodollar futures contract. This contract trades with delivery months up to 10 years in the future and is a futures contract on a 3-month interest rate. The contract is settled in cash. The maturity date is two days before the third Wednesday of the delivery month. The contract is marked to market daily until the maturity date. At that time the settlement price is calculated as 100 minus the three-month LIBOR percentage rate observed in the market. For example, if on the maturity date the 3-month LIBOR rate is 4.80%, the final settlement price is 95.20. A futures contract is structured so that when the futures quote increases by one basis point (e.g. from 95.22 to 95.23) there is a gain of $25 on one long contract.

Because Eurodollar futures contracts are so liquid analysts often use them to estimate forward interest rates. Suppose that the December Eurodollar futures price is 95.00. Does this mean that (with the appropriate compounding frequency and day count conventions) the forward rate for a three month period beginning two days before the third Wednesday of December 2015 is 100 − 95.00 or 5.00%? The answer is that is necessary to make what is termed a "convexity adjustment" to convert the 5.00% to the required forward rate. The convexity adjustment is described in Section 6.3. It increases as the maturity of the futures contract increases. In the example considered in the text it increases from 0 to 73.8 basis points as the contract maturity increases from 0 to 10 years. (See Example 6.4.)

The last part of the chapter covers duration. The duration of an instrument describes its sensitivity to interest rates. Specifically it describes the sensitivity to a small parallel shift in the yield curve. The key equation is equation (6.7) when interest rates are expressed with continuous compounding and equation (6.9) when interest rates are expressed with a compounding frequency of m times per year. Suppose that the duration of an instrument is 4 years and we are considering the effect of a 0.05% increase in all (continuously compounded) interest rates. In this case $D = 4$ and $\Delta y = 0.0005$. Equation (6.7) shows that change in the price of the instrument being considered is 4×0.0005 or 0.002 times the price. This means that the percentage change is 0.2%.

When hedging an interest rate exposure using a futures contract the hedge ratio is determined by a) the duration of the instrument underlying the futures contract at the futures contract maturity and b) the duration of the exposure being hedged at the hedge maturity. For example if the duration of the bond that is expected to be delivered in a Treasury note futures contract is 8 years and the duration of the exposure that is being hedged is 12 years, the hedge ratio should be 1.5; that is the size of the futures position should be 50% greater than the size of the position being hedged (see equation 6.10).

Answers to Practice Questions

Problem 6.8.
The price of a 90-day Treasury bill is quoted as 10.00. What continuously compounded return (on an actual/365 basis) does an investor earn on the Treasury bill for the 90-day period?

The cash price of the Treasury bill is
$$100 - \frac{90}{360} \times 10 = \$97.50$$

The annualized continuously compounded return is
$$\frac{365}{90} \ln\left(1 + \frac{2.5}{97.5}\right) = 10.27\%$$

Problem 6.9.
It is May 5, 2017. The quoted price of a government bond with a 12% coupon that matures on July 27, 2024, is 110-17. What is the cash price?

The number of days between January 27, 2017 and May 5, 2017 is 98. The number of days between January 27, 2017 and July 27, 2017 is 181. The accrued interest is therefore
$$6 \times \frac{98}{181} = 3.2486$$
The quoted price is 110.5312. The cash price is therefore
$$110.5312 + 3.2486 = 113.7798$$
or $113.78.

Problem 6.10.
Suppose that the Treasury bond futures price is 101-12. Which of the following four bonds is cheapest to deliver?

Bond	Price	Conversion Factor
1	125-05	1.2131
2	142-15	1.3792
3	115-31	1.1149
4	144-02	1.4026

The cheapest-to-deliver bond is the one for which

$$Quoted\ Price - Futures\ Price \times Conversion\ Factor$$

is least. Calculating this factor for each of the 4 bonds we get

$$Bond\ 1 : 125.15625 - 101.375 \times 1.2131 = 2.178$$
$$Bond\ 2 : 142.46875 - 101.375 \times 1.3792 = 2.652$$
$$Bond\ 3 : 115.96875 - 101.375 \times 1.1149 = 2.946$$
$$Bond\ 4 : 144.06250 - 101.375 \times 1.4026 = 1.874$$

Bond 4 is therefore the cheapest to deliver.

Problem 6.11.

It is July 30, 2017. The cheapest-to-deliver bond in a September 2017 Treasury bond futures contract is a 13% coupon bond, and delivery is expected to be made on September 30, 2017. Coupon payments on the bond are made on February 4 and August 4 each year. The term structure is flat, and the rate of interest with semiannual compounding is 12% per annum. The conversion factor for the bond is 1.5. The current quoted bond price is $110. Calculate the quoted futures price for the contract.

There are 176 days between February 4 and July 30 and 181 days between February 4 and August 4. The cash price of the bond is, therefore:

$$110 + \frac{176}{181} \times 6.5 = 116.32$$

The rate of interest with continuous compounding is $2\ln 1.06 = 0.1165$ or 11.65% per annum. A coupon of 6.5 will be received in 5 days (= 0.01370 years) time. The present value of the coupon is

$$6.5 e^{-0.01370 \times 0.1165} = 6.49$$

The futures contract lasts for 62 days (= 0.1699 years). The cash futures price if the contract were written on the 13% bond would be

$$(116.32 - 6.49) e^{0.1699 \times 0.1165} = 112.03$$

At delivery there are 57 days of accrued interest. The quoted futures price if the contract were written on the 13% bond would therefore be

$$112.03 - 6.5 \times \frac{57}{184} = 110.01$$

Taking the conversion factor into account the quoted futures price should be:

$$\frac{110.01}{1.5} = 73.34$$

Problem 6.12.

An investor is looking for arbitrage opportunities in the Treasury bond futures market. What complications are created by the fact that the party with a short position can choose to deliver any bond with a maturity between 15 and 25 years?

If the bond to be delivered and the time of delivery were known, arbitrage would be straightforward. When the futures price is too high, the arbitrageur buys bonds and shorts an equivalent number of bond futures contracts. When the futures price is too low, the arbitrageur shorts bonds and goes long an equivalent number of bond futures contracts.

Uncertainty as to which bond will be delivered introduces complications. The bond that appears cheapest-to-deliver now may not in fact be cheapest-to-deliver at maturity. In the case where the futures price is too high, this is not a major problem since the party with the short position (i.e., the arbitrageur) determines which bond is to be delivered. In the case where the futures price is too low, the arbitrageur's position is far more difficult since he or she does not know which bond to short; it is unlikely that a profit can be locked in for all possible outcomes.

Problem 6.13.

Suppose that the nine-month LIBOR interest rate is 8% per annum and the six-month LIBOR interest rate is 7.5% per annum (both with actual/365 and continuous compounding). Estimate the three-month Eurodollar futures price quote for a contract maturing in six months.

The forward interest rate for the time period between months 6 and 9 is 9% per annum with continuous compounding. This is because 9% per annum for three months when combined with $7\frac{1}{2}$% per annum for six months gives an average interest rate of 8% per annum for the nine-month period.

With quarterly compounding the forward interest rate is

$$4(e^{0.09/4} - 1) = 0.09102$$

or 9.102%. This assumes that the day count is actual/365. With a day count of actual/360 the rate is $9.102 \times 360/365 = 8.977$. The three-month Eurodollar quote for a contract maturing in six months is therefore

$$100 - 8.977 = 91.02$$

Problem 6.14.

A five-year bond with a yield of 11% (continuously compounded) pays an 8% coupon at the end of each year.

a) *What is the bond's price?*
b) *What is the bond's duration?*
c) *Use the duration to calculate the effect on the bond's price of a 0.2% decrease in its yield.*
d) *Recalculate the bond's price on the basis of a 10.8% per annum yield and verify that the result is in agreement with your answer to (c).*

a) The bond's price is

$$8e^{-0.11} + 8e^{-0.11 \times 2} + 8e^{-0.11 \times 3} + 8e^{-0.11 \times 4} + 108e^{-0.11 \times 5} = 86.80$$

b) The bond's duration is

$$\frac{1}{86.80}\left[8e^{-0.11}+2\times 8e^{-0.11\times 2}+3\times 8e^{-0.11\times 3}+4\times 8e^{-0.11\times 4}+5\times 108e^{-0.11\times 5}\right]$$

$$=4.256\text{years}$$

c) Since, with the notation in the chapter

$$\Delta B=-BD\Delta y$$

the effect on the bond's price of a 0.2% decrease in its yield is

$$86.80\times 4.256\times 0.002=0.74$$

The bond's price should increase from 86.80 to 87.54.

d) With a 10.8% yield the bond's price is

$$8e^{-0.108}+8e^{-0.108\times 2}+8e^{-0.108\times 3}+8e^{-0.108\times 4}+108e^{-0.108\times 5}=87.54$$

This is consistent with the answer in (c).

Problem 6.15.

Suppose that a bond portfolio with a duration of 12 years is hedged using a futures contract in which the underlying asset has a duration of four years. What is likely to be the impact on the hedge of the fact that the 12-year rate is less volatile than the four-year rate?

Duration-based hedging procedures assume parallel shifts in the yield curve. Since the 12-year rate tends to move by less than the 4-year rate, the portfolio manager may find that he or she is over-hedged.

Problem 6.16.

Suppose that it is February 20 and a treasurer realizes that on July 17 the company will have to issue $5 million of commercial paper with a maturity of 180 days. If the paper were issued today, the company would realize $4,820,000. (In other words, the company would receive $4,820,000 for its paper and have to redeem it at $5,000,000 in 180 days' time.) The September Eurodollar futures price is quoted as 92.00. How should the treasurer hedge the company's exposure?

The company treasurer can hedge the company's exposure by shorting Eurodollar futures contracts. The Eurodollar futures position leads to a profit if rates rise and a loss if they fall. The duration of the commercial paper is twice that of the Eurodollar deposit underlying the Eurodollar futures contract. The contract price of a Eurodollar futures contract is 980,000. The number of contracts that should be shorted is, therefore,

$$\frac{4,820,000}{980,000}\times 2=9.84$$

Rounding to the nearest whole number 10 contracts should be shorted.

Problem 6.17.

On August 1 a portfolio manager has a bond portfolio worth $10 million. The duration of the portfolio in October will be 7.1 years. The December Treasury bond futures price is currently 91-12 and the cheapest-to-deliver bond will have a duration of 8.8 years at maturity. How *should the portfolio manager immunize the portfolio against changes in interest rates over the next two months?*

The treasurer should short Treasury bond futures contract. If bond prices go down, this futures position will provide offsetting gains. The number of contracts that should be shorted is

$$\frac{10,000,000 \times 7.1}{91,375 \times 8.8} = 88.30$$

Rounding to the nearest whole number 88 contracts should be shorted. (Note that it can be argued that the average duration of the portfolio during the life of the hedge should be used instead of the duration of the portfolio at the beginning of the life of the hedge.)

Problem 6.18.
How can the portfolio manager change the duration of the portfolio to 3.0 years in Problem 6.17?

The answer in Problem 6.17 is designed to reduce the duration to zero. To reduce the duration from 7.1 to 3.0 instead of from 7.1 to 0, the treasurer should short

$$\frac{4.1}{7.1} \times 88.30 = 50.99$$

or 51 contracts.

Problem 6.19.
Between October 30, 2017, and November 1, 2017, you have a choice between owning a U.S. government bond paying a 12% coupon and a U.S. corporate bond paying a 12% coupon. Consider carefully the day count conventions discussed in this chapter and decide which of the two bonds you would prefer to own. Ignore the risk of default.

You would prefer to own the Treasury bond. Under the 30/360 day count convention there is one day between October 30 and November 1. Under the actual/actual (in period) day count convention, there are two days. Therefore you would earn approximately twice as much interest by holding the Treasury bond.

Problem 6.20.
Suppose that a Eurodollar futures quote is 88 for a contract maturing in 60 days. What is the LIBOR forward rate for the 60- to 150-day period? Ignore the difference between futures and forwards for the purposes of this question.

The Eurodollar futures contract price of 88 means that the Eurodollar futures rate is 12% per annum. This is the forward rate for the 60- to 150-day period with quarterly compounding and an actual/360 day count convention.

Problem 6.21.
The three-month Eurodollar futures price for a contract maturing in six years is quoted as 95.20. The standard deviation of the change in the short-term interest rate in one year is 1.1%. Estimate the forward LIBOR interest rate for the period between 6.00 and 6.25 years in the future.

Using the notation of Section 6.3, $\sigma = 0.011$, $t_1 = 6$, and $t_2 = 6.25$. The convexity adjustment is

$$\frac{1}{2} \times 0.011^2 \times 6 \times 6.25 = 0.002269$$

or about 23 basis points. The futures rate is 4.8% with quarterly compounding and an actual/360 day count. This becomes $4.8 \times 365/360 = 4.867\%$ with an actual/actual day count. It is $4\ln(1+.04867/4) = 4.84\%$ with continuous compounding. The forward rate is therefore $4.84 - 0.23 = 4.61\%$ with continuous compounding.

Problem 6.22.
Explain why the forward interest rate is less than the corresponding futures interest rate calculated from a Eurodollar futures contract.

Suppose that the contracts apply to the interest rate between times T_1 and T_2. There are two reasons for a difference between the forward rate and the futures rate. The first is that the futures contract is settled daily whereas the forward contract is settled once at time T_2. The second is that without daily settlement a futures contract would be settled at time T_1 not T_2. Both reasons tend to make the futures rate greater than the forward rate.

CHAPTER 7
Swaps

This chapter covers how interest rate swaps and currency swaps work and how they are valued. A plain vanilla interest rate swap is an agreement to exchange interest at a fixed rate for interest at LIBOR. Table 7.1 provides an example of a hypothetical three-year swap between Citigroup and Apple where 3% is paid and six-month LIBOR is received with payments being exchanged every six months. It should be emphasized that Table 7.1 is just an example of what could happen. At the outset, the LIBOR rates that will determine all the swap's cash flows except the first are uncertain. The exchange made on September 8, 2016 is known on March 8, 2016 when the swap is initiated. The other exchanges depend on the LIBOR rates at future times. Note that, in a "plain vanilla" interest rate swap where six-month LIBOR is exchanged for fixed, the six-month LIBOR rate observed on a date determines the cash flows exchanged six months later.

An interest rate swap can be used to transform an asset or a liability. A swap where fixed is received and floating is paid can be used to convert a liability where a company is paying a fixed rate of interest to one where it is paying a floating rate of interest. The same swap can be used to convert an asset earning a floating rate of interest to an asset earning a fixed rate of interest. A swap where floating is received and fixed is paid can be used to convert a liability where a company is paying a floating rate of interest to one where it is paying a fixed rate of interest. The same swap can be used to convert an asset earning a fixed rate of interest to an asset earning a floating rate of interest. This is illustrated in Figures 7.2, 7.4, 7.5, and 7.6.

You should make sure you understand Table 7.3 and Business Snapshot 7.1. Table 7.3 shows quotes as they might be made by a swap market maker such as Goldman Sachs and Business Snapshot 7.1 shows an extract from a confirmation for a hypothetical bilaterally traded swap.

The comparative advantage argument is sometimes used in an attempt to persuade corporate treasurers to enter into swaps. It is a superficially compelling argument. It says that companies should borrow in the market where they have (or appear to have) a comparative advantage. They should then use swaps to exchange the liability for what they want. In the case of currency swaps, as discussed in Section 7.7, this type of argument can have some validity because of tax effects. However, as discussed in Section 7.4, in the case of interest rate swaps it is seriously flawed because it ignores the possibility of a company's creditworthiness declining so that the spread over LIBOR at which it borrows increases.

As explained in Section 4.2, a swap rate is a low-credit-risk interest rate. For example the five-year swap rate corresponds to the rate earned by a financial institution when it lends a certain sum for six-months to a AA-rated company and then relends it for nine further six-month periods ensuring that in each case the borrower has an AA-rating at the beginning of the six-month period. The five-year swap rate is less than the five-year borrowing rate for a AA-rated company because a company that is AA-rated today may be downgraded during the five-year period.

As explained in Section 7.5, the valuation of interest rate swaps involves estimating forward interest rates and calculating the present value of cash flows on the assumption that the forward interest rates will happen. (See Example 7.1.) Traditionally discounting has been done at zero rates calculated from LIBOR and swap rates. It is now standard practice to discount cash flows at OIS zero rates. The OIS zero curve is bootstrapped as explained in Section 4.7. LIBOR forward rates are determined from swap rates as described in Section 7.5 and Example 7.2.

A fixed-for-fixed currency swap is an agreement to exchange a fixed rate in one currency for a fixed rate in another currency. It can be used to transform borrowings in one currency to borrowings in another currency or to transform an asset earning interest in one currency to an asset earning interest in another currency. It can be valued either in terms on bonds or in terms of forward foreign exchange agreements. Examples 7.3 and 7.4 illustrate this.

Swap transactions entail a small amount of credit risk. A swap has zero value when it is first negotiated. As time passes, its value is liable to become positive or negative. The credit exposure to a company from a swap (i.e., the amount it could lose if the counterparty defaults) is $\max(V, 0)$ where V is the value of the swap to the company. This assumes no collateral is posted by the counterparty and there are no other transactions between the company and its counterparty. Part of the spread earned by a swap market marker (see Table 7.3) is to compensate for potential defaults by its counterparties.

Many different types of swaps are traded in practice. The final part of the chapter introduces you to some of the more important swap products. These are discussed further in Chapter 22.

Software

In DG400f.xls, the Swap_Price worksheet allows you to calculate the value of a swap from OIS zeroes and LIBOR forwards. The swap displayed when you first open the worksheet shows how data is input for Example 7.1.

Answers to Practice Questions

Problem 7.8.
A bank enters into an interest rate swap with a nonfinancial counterparty using bilaterally clearing where it is paying a fixed rate of 3% and receiving LIBOR. No collateral is posted and no other transactions are outstanding between the bank and the counterparty. What credit risk is the bank subject to? Discuss whether the credit risk is greater when the yield curve is upward sloping or when it is downward sloping.

At the start of the swap, the contract has a value of approximately zero. As time passes, it is likely that the swap value will change. If at the time of a counterparty default the swap has a positive value to the bank and a negative value to the counterparty, the bank is likely to lose money. If the yield curve is upward sloping, the early exchanges are expected to be negative to the bank and the later exchanges are expected to be positive to the bank. This means that the swap is expected to have a positive value as time passes and, as a result, the bank's credit exposure is relatively high. When the yield curve is downward sloping the early exchanges are expected to be positive to the bank and the later exchanges are expected to be negative to the bank. This means that the swap is expected to have a negative value as time passes and, as a result, the bank's credit exposure is relatively low.

Problem 7.9.
Companies X and Y have been offered the following rates per annum on a $5 million 10-year investment:

	Fixed Rate	Floating Rate
Company X	8.0%	LIBOR
Company Y	8.8%	LIBOR

Company X requires a fixed-rate investment; company Y requires a floating-rate investment. Design a swap that will net a bank, acting as intermediary, 0.2% per annum and will appear equally attractive to X and Y.

The spread between the interest rates offered to X and Y is 0.8% per annum on fixed rate investments and 0.0% per annum on floating rate investments. This means that the total apparent benefit to all parties from the swap is 0.8% per annum. Of this 0.2% per annum will go to the bank. This leaves 0.3% per annum for each of X and Y. In other words, company X should be able to get a fixed-rate return of 8.3% per annum while company Y should be able to get a floating-rate return LIBOR + 0.3% per annum. The required swap is shown in Figure S7.1. The bank earns 0.2%, company X earns 8.3%, and company Y earns LIBOR + 0.3%.

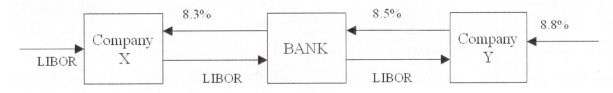

Figure S7.1 Swap for Problem 7.9

Problem 7.10.
A financial institution has entered into an interest rate swap with company X. Under the terms of the swap, it receives 4% per annum and pays six-month LIBOR on a principal of $10 million for five years. Payments are made every six months. Suppose that company X defaults on the sixth payment date (end of year 3) when the six-month forward LIBOR rates for all maturities are 2% per annum. What is the loss to the financial institution? Assume that six-month LIBOR was 3% per annum halfway through year 3 and that at the time of default all OIS rates are 1.8% per annum. OIS rates are expressed with continuous compounding; other rates are expressed with semiannual compounding.

At the end of year 3 the financial institution was due to receive $200,000 (=0.5×4% of $10 million) and pay $150,000 (=0.5×3% of $10 million). The immediate loss is therefore $50,000. To value the remaining swap we assume that LIBOR forward rates are realized. All forward rates are 2% per annum. The remaining cash flows are therefore valued on the assumption that the floating payment is 0.5×0.02×10,000,000 = $100,000. The fixed payment is $200,000 and the net payment that would be received is 200,000−100,000=$100,000. The total cost of default is

43

therefore the cost of foregoing the following cash flows:

3 year:	$50,000
3.5 year:	$100,000
4 year:	$100,000
4.5 year:	$100,000
5 year:	$100,000

Discounting these cash flows to year 3 at 1.8% per annum, we obtain the cost of the default as $441,120.

Problem 7.11.

A financial institution has entered into a 10-year currency swap with company Y. Under the terms of the swap, the financial institution receives interest at 3% per annum in Swiss francs and pays interest at 8% per annum in U.S. dollars. Interest payments are exchanged once a year. The principal amounts are 7 million dollars and 10 million francs. Suppose that company Y declares bankruptcy at the end of year 6, when the exchange rate is $0.80 per franc. What is the cost to the financial institution? Assume that, at the end of year 6, the risk-free interest rate is 3% per annum in Swiss francs and 8% per annum in U.S. dollars for all maturities. All interest rates are quoted with annual compounding.

When interest rates are compounded annually

$$F_0 = S_0 \left(\frac{1+r}{1+r_f} \right)^T$$

where F_0 is the T-year forward rate, S_0 is the spot rate, r is the domestic risk-free rate, and r_f is the foreign risk-free rate. As $r = 0.08$ and $r_f = 0.03$, the spot and forward exchange rates at the end of year 6 are

Spot:	0.8000
1 year forward:	0.8388
2 year forward:	0.8796
3 year forward:	0.9223
4 year forward:	0.9670

The value of the swap at the time of the default can be calculated on the assumption that forward rates are realized. The cash flows lost as a result of the default are therefore as follows:

Year	Dollar Paid	CHF Received	Forward Rate	Dollar Equiv of CHF Received	Cash Flow Lost
6	560,000	300,000	0.8000	240,000	-320,000
7	560,000	300,000	0.8388	251,600	-308,400
8	560,000	300,000	0.8796	263,900	-296,100
9	560,000	300,000	0.9223	276,700	-283,300
10	7,560,000	10,300,000	0.9670	9,960,100	2,400,100

Discounting the numbers in the final column to the end of year 6 at 8% per annum, the cost of the default is $679,800.

Note that, if company Y had no other business beside this swap, it would make no sense for the company to default just before the exchange of payments at the end of year 6 as the exchange has a positive value to company Y. In practice, company Y may be defaulting and declaring bankruptcy for reasons unrelated to this particular transaction.

Problem 7.12.

Companies A and B face the following interest rates (adjusted for the differential impact of taxes):

	A	*B*
US Dollars (floating rate)	*LIBOR+0.5%*	*LIBOR+1.0%*
Canadian dollars (fixed rate)	*5.0%*	*6.5%*

Assume that A wants to borrow U.S. dollars at a floating rate of interest and B wants to borrow Canadian dollars at a fixed rate of interest. A financial institution is planning to arrange a swap and requires a 50-basis-point spread. If the swap is equally attractive to A and B, what rates of interest will A and B end up paying?

Company A has a comparative advantage in the Canadian dollar fixed-rate market. Company B has a comparative advantage in the U.S. dollar floating-rate market. (This may be because of their tax positions.) However, company A wants to borrow in the U.S. dollar floating-rate market and company B wants to borrow in the Canadian dollar fixed-rate market. This gives rise to the swap opportunity.

The differential between the U.S. dollar floating rates is 0.5% per annum, and the differential between the Canadian dollar fixed rates is 1.5% per annum. The difference between the differentials is 1% per annum. The total potential gain to all parties from the swap is therefore 1% per annum, or 100 basis points. If the financial intermediary requires 50 basis points, each of A and B can be made 25 basis points better off. Thus a swap can be designed so that it provides A with U.S. dollars at LIBOR + 0.25% per annum, and B with Canadian dollars at 6.25% per annum. The swap is shown in Figure S7.2.

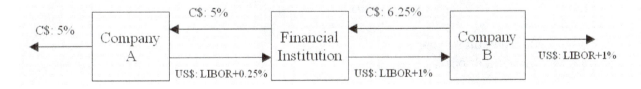

Figure S7.2 Swap for Problem 7.12

Principal payments flow in the opposite direction to the arrows at the start of the life of the swap and in the same direction as the arrows at the end of the life of the swap. The financial institution would be exposed to some foreign exchange risk which could be hedged using forward contracts.

Problem 7.13.

After it hedges its foreign exchange risk using forward contracts, is the financial institution's average spread in Figure 7.11 likely to be greater than or less than 20 basis points? Explain your answer.

The financial institution will have to buy 1.1% of the AUD principal in the forward market for each year of the life of the swap. Since AUD interest rates are higher than dollar interest rates, AUD is at a discount in forward markets. This means that the AUD purchased for year 2 is less expensive than that purchased for year 1; the AUD purchased for year 3 is less expensive than that purchased for year 2; and so on. This works in favor of the financial institution and means that its spread increases with time. The spread is always above 20 basis points.

Problem 7.14.

"Nonfinancial companies with high credit risks are the ones that cannot access fixed-rate markets directly. They are the companies that are most likely to be paying fixed and receiving floating in an interest rate swap." Assume that this statement is true. Do you think it increases or decreases the risk of a financial institution's swap portfolio? Assume that companies are most likely to default when interest rates are high.

Consider two offsetting plain-vanilla interest rate swaps that a financial institution enters into with companies X and Y. We suppose that X is paying fixed and receiving floating while Y is paying floating and receiving fixed.

The quote suggests that company X will usually be less creditworthy than company Y. (Company X might be a BBB-rated company that has difficulty in accessing fixed-rate markets directly; company Y might be a AAA-rated company that has no difficulty accessing fixed or floating rate markets.) Presumably company X wants fixed-rate funds and company Y wants floating-rate funds.

The financial institution will realize a loss if company Y defaults when rates are high or if company X defaults when rates are low. These events are relatively unlikely since (a) Y is unlikely to default in any circumstances and (b) defaults are less likely to happen when rates are low. For the purposes of illustration, suppose that the probabilities of various events are as follows:

Default by Y:	0.001
Default by X:	0.010
Rates high when default occurs:	0.7
Rates low when default occurs:	0.3

The probability of a loss is
$$0.001 \times 0.7 + 0.010 \times 0.3 = 0.0037$$

If the roles of X and Y in the swap had been reversed the probability of a loss would be
$$0.001 \times 0.3 + 0.010 \times 0.7 = 0.0073$$

Assuming companies are more likely to default when interest rates are high, the above argument shows that the observation in quotes has the effect of decreasing the risk of a financial institution's swap portfolio. It is worth noting that the assumption that defaults are more likely when interest rates are high is open to question. The assumption is motivated by the thought that high interest rates often lead to financial difficulties for corporations. However, the empirical evidence on whether defaults are more likely when interest rates are high is mixed.

Problem 7.15.
Why is the expected loss to a bank from a default on a swap less than the expected loss from the default on a loan to the counterparty with the same principal? Assume no other transactions between the bank and the counterparty, that the swap is cleared bilaterally, and that no collateral is provided by the counterparty in the case of either the swap or the loan..

In an interest-rate swap a financial institution's exposure depends on the difference between a fixed-rate of interest and a floating-rate of interest. It has no exposure to the notional principal. In a loan the whole principal can be lost.

Problem 7.16.
A bank finds that its assets are not matched with its liabilities. It is taking floating-rate deposits and making fixed-rate loans. How can swaps be used to offset the risk?

The bank is paying a floating-rate on the deposits and receiving a fixed-rate on the loans. It can offset its risk by entering into interest rate swaps (with other financial institutions or corporations) in which it contracts to pay fixed and receive floating.

Problem 7.17.
Explain how you would value a swap that is the exchange of a floating rate in one currency for a fixed rate in another currency.

Suppose that floating payments are made in currency A and fixed payments are made in currency B. The floating payments can be valued in currency A by (i) assuming that the forward rates are realized, and (ii) discounting the resulting cash flows at appropriate currency A discount rates. Suppose that the value is V_A. The fixed payments can be valued in currency B by discounting them at the appropriate currency B discount rates. Suppose that the value is V_B. If Q is the current exchange rate (number of units of currency A per unit of currency B), the value of the swap in currency A is $V_A - QV_B$. Alternatively, it is $V_A/Q - V_B$ in currency B.

Problem 7.18
OIS rates have been estimated as 3.4% for all maturities. The three-month LIBOR rate is 3.5%. For a six-month swap where payments are exchanged every three months the swap rate is 3.6%. All rates are expressed with quarterly compounding. What is the LIBOR forward rate for the three-month to six-month period?

Suppose that the LIBOR forward rate is F. Assume a principal of $1000. A swap where 3.6% ($9 per quarter) is received and LIBOR is paid is worth zero. The exchange at the three-month point to the party receiving fixed is worth

$$\frac{9 - 1000 \times 0.035/4}{1 + 0.034/4} = 0.2479$$

The exchange at the six-month point to the party receiving fixed is worth

$$\frac{9-1000\times F/4}{(1+0.034/4)^2}$$

Hence

$$\frac{9-1000\times F/4}{(1+0.034/4)^2}+0.2479=0$$

so that $F = 3.701\%$.

Problem 7.19

Six-month LIBOR is 5%. LIBOR forward rates for the 6- to 12-month period and for the 12- to 18-month period are both 5.5%. Swap rates for 2- and 3-year semiannual pay swaps are 5.4% and 5.6%, respectively. Estimate the LIBOR forward rates for maturities of 18-month to 2 years, 2 to 2.5 years, and 2.5 to 3 years. Assume that the 2.5-year swap rate is the average of the 2- and 3-year swap rates and that OIS zero rates for all maturities are 4.5%. OIS rates are expressed with continuous compounding; all other rates are expressed with semiannual compounding.

Suppose the 18-month to 2-year forward rate is F. The two-year swap rate is 5.4%. Setting the value of the two-year swap equal to zero:

$(0.05-0.054)e^{-0.045\times0.5} + (0.055-0.054)\, e^{-0.045\times1.0} + (0.055-0.054)\, e^{-0.045\times1.5}$
$+(F-0.054)e^{-0.045\times2} = 0$

which gives $F = 0.0562$. The 18-month to two-year forward LIBOR rate is therefore 5.62%.

Suppose next that the 2-year to 2.5-year forward rate is F. The 2.5 year swap rate is 5.5%. Setting the value of the 2.5 year swap equal to zero:

$(0.05-0.055)e^{-0.045\times0.5} + (0.055-0.055)\, e^{-0.045\times1.0} + (0.055-0.055)\, e^{-0.045\times1.5}$
$+(0.0562-0.055)e^{-0.045\times2} +(F-0.055)\, e^{-0.045\times2.5} = 0$

which gives $F = 0.0592$. The 2- to 2.5-year forward LIBOR rate is therefore 5.92%.

Suppose next that the 2.5-year to 3-year forward rate is F. The three-year swap rate is 5.6%. Setting the value of the 3-year swap equal to zero:

$(0.05-0.056)e^{-0.045\times0.5} + (0.055-0.056)\, e^{-0.045\times1.0} + (0.055-0.056)\, e^{-0.045\times1.5}$
$+(0.0562-0.056)e^{-0.045\times2} +(0.0592-0.056)\, e^{-0.045\times2.5} + (F-0.056)\, e^{-0.045\times3} = 0$

which gives $F = 0.0614$. The 2.5- to 3-year forward LIBOR rate is therefore 6.14%.

CHAPTER 8
Securitization and the Credit Crisis of 2007

This chapter covers issues arising from the credit crisis that started in 2007. It explains how securitization works, describes what happened to the US real estate market before and after the crisis, discusses the lessons that can be learned, and outlines the regulations that have been put in place in an attempt to prevent future crises

There are two securities you should understand: ABSs and ABS CDOs. There are two ways of describing how these securities work. One is in terms of the waterfall (see Figure 8.2): cash flows go first to the most senior tranche, then to the next-most-senior tranche, and so on. The other is in terms of who bears the losses: losses are borne first by the most junior tranche, then by the next-most-junior tranche, and so on. The ABS tranches we are concerned with were created from a portfolio of subprime mortgages. ABS CDO tranches were created from a portfolio of tranches, each from a different ABS. Make sure you understand how Table 8.1 is calculated from Figure 8.3.

The subprime story in Section 8.2 is fairly simple. Lenders relaxed their criteria for granting mortgages. More people were able to borrow money to buy their first home. The demand for houses increased. House prices therefore increased. When people found they could not afford their mortgages, there were foreclosures. The supply of houses then exceeded the demand and prices decreased. This led to losses on the ABSs and ABS CDOs that were created from mortgages. Investors panicked and moved to safe securities such as Treasury bonds and credit spreads increased. Banks that had invested in the tranches of ABSs and ABS CDOs lost a great deal of money.

Not surprisingly, it is taking some time to sort out the resulting mess. There have been many proposals to change the regulations that govern the way banks and other financial institutions operate. It is now realized that mistakes were made during the period leading up to the crisis (see Section 8.3). As explained in Section 8.4, the over-the-counter derivatives markets has been subject to a lot of regulation since the crisis; proprietary trading by banks is now restricted, banks have to keep more equity capital, and regulations have been introduced to ensure that their liquidity is satisfactory.

Answers to Practice Questions

Problem 8.8.
Why did mortgage lenders frequently not check on information provided by potential borrowers on mortgage application forms during the 2000 to 2007 period?

Subprime mortgages were frequently securitized. The only information that was retained during the securitization process was the applicant's FICO score and the loan-to-value ratio of the mortgage.

Problem 8.9.
How were the risks in ABS CDOs misjudged by the market?

Investors underestimated how high the default correlations between mortgages would be in stressed market conditions. Investors also did not always realize that the tranches underlying ABS CDOs were usually quite thin so that they were either totally wiped out or untouched. There was an unfortunate tendency to assume that a tranche with a particular rating could be considered to be the same as a bond with that rating. This assumption is not valid for the reasons just mentioned.

Problem 8.10.

What is meant by the term "agency costs"? How did agency costs play a role in the credit crisis?

"Agency costs" is a term used to describe the costs in a situation where the interests of two parties are not perfectly aligned. As described at the end of Section 8.3, the interests of valuers, mortgage originators, the creators of ABS and ABS CDO structures, the investors in the structures, traders, and the financial institutions for which traders worked were not perfectly aligned.

Problem 8.11.

How is an ABS CDO created? What was the motivation to create ABS CDOs?

An ABS CDO was frequently created from the BBB-rated tranches of ABSs. This is because it was difficult to sell the BBB-rated tranches of an ABS to investors in a direct way.

Problem 8.12.

Explain the impact of an increase in default correlation on the risks of the senior tranche of an ABS. What is its impact on the risks of the equity tranche?

Consider the structure in Figure 8.1. Assume that there are 1000 assets each with a principal of $100,000. Suppose that all the assets have a 5% chance of defaulting during the life of the ABS and there will be a 50% recovery. For the senior tranche to be affected there have to be at least 400 defaults. When default correlation is zero there is virtually no chance of this. As default correlation increases, 400 defaults becomes more likely. In the limit as the correlation approaches one there is a 5% chance that all 1000 will default.
As default correlation increases, the equity tranche becomes less risky. When the default correlation is low some defaults are almost certain to happen so that the equity tranche experiences losses. As the default correlation increases it becomes less likely that there will be defaults. In the limit as the correlation approaches one there is a 95% chance that there will be no defaults and the equity tranche experiences no losses.

Problem 8.13.

Explain why the AAA-rated tranche of an ABS CDO is more risky than the AAA-rated tranche of an ABS.

As indicated in Table 8.1, a moderately high loss rate will wipe out the mezzanine tranches of ABSs so that the AAA-rated tranche of the ABS CDO is also wiped out. A moderately high loss rate will at worst wipe out only part of the AAA-rated tranche of an ABS.

Problem 8.14.
Explain why the end-of-year bonus is sometimes referred to as "short-term compensation."

The end-of-year bonus usually reflects performance during the year. This type of compensation tends to lead traders and other employees of banks to focus on their next bonus and therefore have a short-term time horizon for their decision making.

Problem 8.15.
Add rows in Table 8.1 corresponding to losses on the underlying assets of (a) 2%, (b) 6%, (c) 14%, and (d) 18%.

Losses to subprime portfolio	Losses to Mezz tranche of ABS	Losses to equity tranche of ABS CDO	Losses to Mezz tranche of ABS CDO	Losses to senior tranche of ABS CDO
2%	0%	0%	0%	0%
6%	6.7%	67%	0%	0%
14%	60.0%	100%	100%	38.5%
18%	86.7%	100%	100%	79.5%

CHAPTER 9
Mechanics of Options Markets

If you already understand how options work you will not have to spend a lot of time on Chapter 9. Bear in mind that, for every trader buying an option, there is another trader selling it. Make sure you understand the profit diagrams in Figures 9.1 to 9.4. Figure 9.5 shows the payoffs from the four different option strategies in Figures 9.1 to 9.4. Whereas the profit takes account of the initial amount paid for the option, the payoff does not.

Make sure you understand the terminology of option markets: American options, European options, strike price, expiration date, intrinsic value, option class, option series, in-the-money, at-the-money, out-of-the-money, flex options, option writing, and so on.

Except in special circumstances (see for example Business Snapshot 9.1), there is no adjustment to the terms of an option for cash dividends. Stock dividends and stock splits do lead to adjustments. For example, a 3-for-1 stock split leads to the strike price being reduced to a third of what it was before and the number of options held being multiplied by 3. A 10% stock dividend is like a 1.1 for 1 stock split. It leads to the strike price being reduced to 10/11 of what it was before and the number of options held being increased by 10%.

Traders who sell (i.e., write) options must maintain margin accounts similar to the margin accounts for futures traders. Traders who buy options usually pay for the options up front and do not maintain margin accounts.

Warrants issued by a company on its own stock are different from regular call options in that exercise of the warrants leads to the company issuing more shares. (When a regular call option on a stock is exercised, the option writer buys shares of the stock in the market and delivers them to the option holder.) Employee stock options and convertible bonds are similar to warrants in this respect.

Options trade in the over-the-counter market as well as on exchanges. Indeed, for many types of underlying (e.g., exchange rates and interest rates) the over-the-counter market is much bigger than the exchange-traded market. The options traded over the counter do not have to have the standard terms defined by exchanges. The terms can be chosen to meet the precise needs of corporate treasurers and fund managers. Sometimes the options have a different structure from regular options. They are then referred to as exotic options (or just exotics). Exotic options are discussed in Chapter 22. Some of the non-standard options traded by the CBOE are discussed in Section 9.4.

Answers to Practice Questions

Problem 9.8.
A corporate treasurer is designing a hedging program involving foreign currency options. What are the pros and cons of using (a) the NASDAQ OMX and (b) the over-the-counter market for

trading?

The NASDAQ OMX offers options with standard strike prices and times to maturity. Options in the over-the-counter market have the advantage that they can be tailored to meet the precise needs of the treasurer. Their disadvantage is that they expose the treasurer to some credit risk. Exchanges organize their trading so that there is virtually no credit risk.

Problem 9.9.

Suppose that a European call option to buy a share for $100.00 costs $5.00 and is held until maturity. Under what circumstances will the holder of the option make a profit? Under what circumstances will the option be exercised? Draw a diagram illustrating how the profit from a long position in the option depends on the stock price at maturity of the option.

Ignoring the time value of money, the holder of the option will make a profit if the stock price at maturity of the option is greater than $105. This is because the payoff to the holder of the option is, in these circumstances, greater than the $5 paid for the option. The option will be exercised if the stock price at maturity is greater than $100. Note that if the stock price is between $100 and $105 the option is exercised, but the holder of the option takes a loss overall. The profit from a long position is as shown in Figure S9.1.

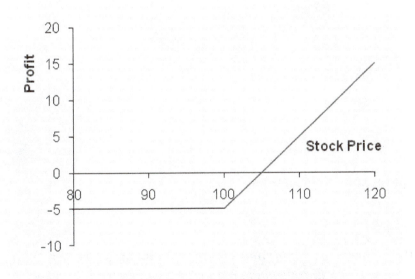

Figure S9.1   Profit from long position in Problem 9.9

Problem 9.10.

Suppose that a European put option to sell a share for $60 costs $8 and is held until maturity. Under what circumstances will the seller of the option (the party with the short position) make a profit? Under what circumstances will the option be exercised? Draw a diagram illustrating how the profit from a short position in the option depends on the stock price at maturity of the option.

Ignoring the time value of money, the seller of the option will make a profit if the stock price at maturity is greater than $52.00. This is because the cost to the seller of the option is in these circumstances less than the price received for the option. The option will be exercised if the stock price at maturity is less than $60.00. Note that if the stock price is between $52.00 and $60.00 the seller of the option makes a profit even though the option is exercised. The profit from the short position is as shown in Figure S9.2.

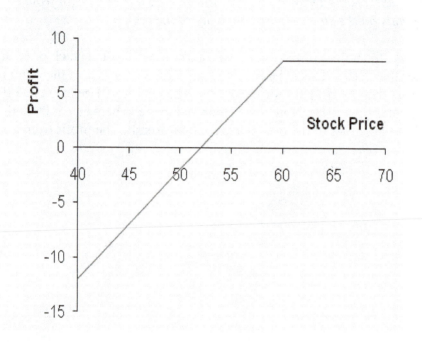

Figure S9.2   Profit from short position in Problem 9.10

Problem 9.11.

Describe the terminal value of the following portfolio: a newly entered-into long forward contract on an asset and a long position in a European put option on the asset with the same maturity as the forward contract and a strike price that is equal to the forward price of the asset at the time the portfolio is set up. Show that the European put option has the same value as a European call option with the same strike price and maturity.

The terminal value of the long forward contract is:

$$S_T - F_0$$

where S_T is the price of the asset at maturity and F_0 is the forward price of the asset at the time the portfolio is set up. (The delivery price in the forward contract is also F_0.)

The terminal value of the put option is:

$$\max(F_0 - S_T, 0)$$

The terminal value of the portfolio is therefore

$$S_T - F_0 + \max(F_0 - S_T, 0)$$
$$= \max(0, S_T - F_0]$$

This is the same as the terminal value of a European call option with the same maturity as the forward contract and an exercise price equal to F_0. This result is illustrated in the Figure S9.3.

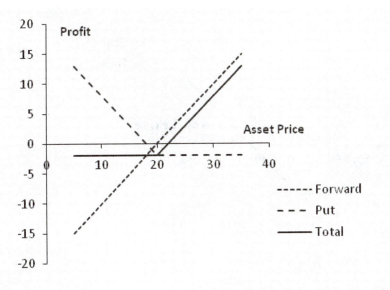

Figure S9.3   Profit from portfolio in Problem 9.11

We have shown that the forward contract plus the put is worth the same as a call with the same strike price and time to maturity as the put. The forward contract is worth zero at the time the portfolio is set up. It follows that the put is worth the same as the call at the time the portfolio is set up.

Problem 9.12.
A trader buys a call option with a strike price of $45 and a put option with a strike price of $40. Both options have the same maturity. The call costs $3 and the put costs $4. Draw a diagram showing the variation of the trader's profit with the asset price.

Figure S9.4 shows the variation of the trader's position with the asset price. We can divide the alternative asset prices into three ranges:
a)   When the asset price less than $40, the put option provides a payoff of $40 - S_T$ and the call option provides no payoff. The options cost $7 and so the total profit is $33 - S_T$.
b)   When the asset price is between $40 and $45, neither option provides a payoff. There is a net loss of $7.
c)   When the asset price greater than $45, the call option provides a payoff of $S_T - 45$ and the

put option provides no payoff. Taking into account the $7 cost of the options, the total profit is $S_T - 52$.

The trader makes a profit (ignoring the time value of money) if the stock price is less than $33 or greater than $52. This type of trading strategy is known as a strangle and is discussed in Chapter 11.

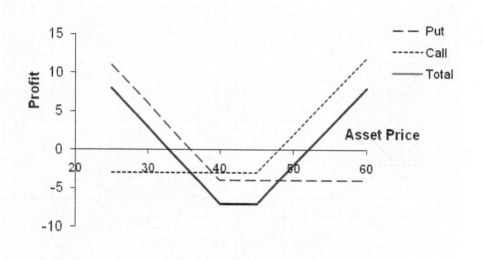

Figure S9.4   Profit from trading strategy in Problem 9.12

Problem 9.13.
Explain why an American option is always worth at least as much as a European option on the same asset with the same strike price and exercise date.

The holder of an American option has all the same rights as the holder of a European option and more. It must therefore be worth at least as much. If it were not, an arbitrageur could short the European option and take a long position in the American option.

Problem 9.14.
Explain why an American option is always worth at least as much as its intrinsic value.

The holder of an American option has the right to exercise it immediately. The American option must therefore be worth at least as much as its intrinsic value. If it were not an arbitrageur could lock in a sure profit by buying the option and exercising it immediately.

Problem 9.15.
Explain carefully the difference between writing a put option and buying a call option.

Writing a put gives a payoff of $\min(S_T - K, 0)$. Buying a call gives a payoff of $\max(S_T - K, 0)$. In both cases the potential payoff is $S_T - K$. The difference is that for a written put the counterparty chooses whether you get the payoff (and will allow you to get it only when it is negative to you). For a long call you decide whether you get the payoff (and you choose to get it when it is positive to you.)

Problem 9.16.
The treasurer of a corporation is trying to choose between options and forward contracts to hedge the corporation's foreign exchange risk. Discuss the advantages and disadvantages of each.

Forward contracts lock in the exchange rate that will apply to a particular transaction in the future. Options provide insurance that the exchange rate will not be worse than some level. The advantage of a forward contract is that uncertainty is eliminated as far as possible. The disadvantage is that the outcome with hedging can be significantly worse than the outcome with no hedging. This disadvantage is not as marked with options. However, unlike forward contracts, options involve an up-front cost.

Problem 9.17.
Consider an exchange-traded call option contract to buy 500 shares with a strike price of $40 and maturity in four months. Explain how the terms of the option contract change when there is
  a) *A 10% stock dividend*
  b) *A 10% cash dividend*
  c) *A 4-for-1 stock split*

a) The option contract becomes one to buy $500 \times 1.1 = 550$ shares with an exercise price $40/1.1 = 36.36$.
b) There is no effect. The terms of an options contract are not normally adjusted for cash dividends.
c) The option contract becomes one to buy $500 \times 4 = 2,000$ shares with an exercise price of 40/4=$10.

Problem 9.18.
"If most of the call options on a stock are in the money, it is likely that the stock price has risen rapidly in the last few months." Discuss this statement.

The exchange has certain rules governing when trading in a new option is initiated. These mean that the option is close-to-the-money when it is first traded. If all call options are in the money, it is therefore likely that the stock price has risen since trading in the option began.

Problem 9.19.
What is the effect of an unexpected cash dividend on (a) a call option price and (b) a put option price?

An unexpected cash dividend would reduce the stock price on the ex-dividend date. This stock price reduction would not be anticipated by option holders prior to the dividend announcement. As a result there would be a reduction in the value of a call option and an increase the value of a put option. (Note that the terms of an option are adjusted for cash dividends only in exceptional circumstances.)

Problem 9.20.

Options on General Motors stock are on a March, June, September, and December cycle. What options trade on (a) March 1, (b) June 30, and (c) August 5?

a) March, April, June and September
b) July, August, September, December
c) August, September, December, March.

Longer dated options may also trade.

Problem 9.21.

Explain why the market maker's bid-offer spread represents a real cost to options investors.

A "fair" price for the option can reasonably be assumed to be half way between the bid and the offer price quoted by a market maker. An investor typically buys at the market maker's offer and sells at the market maker's bid. Each time he or she does this there is a hidden cost equal to half the bid-offer spread.

Problem 9.22.

A U.S. investor writes five naked call option contracts. The option price is $3.50, the strike price is $60.00, and the stock price is $57.00. What is the initial margin requirement?

The two calculations are necessary to determine the initial margin. The first gives
$$500 \times (3.5 + 0.2 \times 57 - 3) = 5,950$$

The second gives

$$500 \times (3.5 + 0.1 \times 57) = 4,600$$

The initial margin is the greater of these, or $5,950. Part of this can be provided by the initial amount of 500×3.5 = $1,750 received for the options.

CHAPTER 10
Properties of Stock Options

This chapter starts by considering the general way in which an option price depends on the stock price, strike price, time to expiration, volatility, risk-free rate, and dividends. Make sure you understand Table 10.1. An important point that often causes confusion is that Table 10.1 considers the change in a variable with all the other variables remaining the same. (This the assumption in calculus when partial derivatives are calculated.) For example, when considering interest rates it is assumed that interest rates change without any other variables changing; the fact that interest rate increases (decreases) tend to be accompanied by stock price decreases (increases) is not considered.

The rest of the chapter considers what we can say about option prices without making any assumptions about volatility or the way in which the stock price behaves. The arguments used are no-arbitrage arguments. Section 10.3, for example, derives upper and lower bounds for call and put options. If the price of an option is outside the range given by the upper and lower bound there is a clear arbitrage opportunity. For example, if a call option price is below the lower bound an arbitrageur buys the option and shorts the stock; if it is above the upper bound the arbitrageur buys the stock and sells the option.

Put-call parity (see equations 10.6 and 10.10) is a very important result. It shows that there is a relationship between the price of a European call option with a certain strike price and time to maturity and the price of a European put option with the same strike price and time to maturity. As illustrated in Table 10.3 there is an arbitrage opportunity if put-call parity does not hold. For American options, put-call parity does not hold, but an inequality relationship can be derived (see equations 10.7 and 10.11).

An American call option on a stock that will not pay dividends during the life of the option should never be exercised early. This is because a) delaying exercise has the advantage that it delays paying the strike price and b) exercising early would give up the protection that the option holder has against the possibility of the stock price falling below the strike price by the end of the life of the option. American put options on stocks that do not pay a dividend are liable to be exercised early. Indeed, it can be shown that at any given time there is always a critical stock price below which it is optimal for the holder of the put option to exercise.

Software

If you are keen to price options at this stage, you can do this in DG400f.xls by using the worksheet Equity_FX_Indx_Fut_Opts_Calc. Choose Equity as the Underlying Type and Black_Scholes – European as the Option Type. Do not check the Implied Volatility box. The timing and amount of dividends can be entered in the table and the software allows you to value a call or put option in terms of the six key variables introduced in this chapter.

Answers to Practice Questions

Problem 10.8.
Explain why the arguments leading to put–call parity for European options cannot be used to give a similar result for American options.

When early exercise is not possible, we can argue that two portfolios that are worth the same at time T must be worth the same at earlier times. When early exercise is possible, the argument is no longer valid. Suppose that $P + S > C + Ke^{-rT}$. This situation does not lead to an arbitrage opportunity. If we buy the call, short the put, and short the stock, we cannot be sure of the result because we do not know when the put will be exercised.

Problem 10.9.
What is a lower bound for the price of a six-month call option on a non-dividend-paying stock when the stock price is $80, the strike price is $75, and the risk-free interest rate is 10% per annum?

The lower bound is

$$80 - 75e^{-0.1 \times 0.5} = \$8.66$$

Problem 10.10
What is a lower bound for the price of a two-month European put option on a non-dividend-paying stock when the stock price is $58, the strike price is $65, and the risk-free interest rate is 5% per annum?

The lower bound is

$$65e^{-0.05 \times 2/12} - 58 = \$6.46$$

Problem 10.11.
A four-month European call option on a dividend-paying stock is currently selling for $5. The stock price is $64, the strike price is $60, and a dividend of $0.80 is expected in one month. The risk-free interest rate is 12% per annum for all maturities. What opportunities are there for an arbitrageur?

The present value of the strike price is $60e^{-0.12 \times 4/12} = \$57.65$. The present value of the dividend is $0.80e^{-0.12 \times 1/12} = 0.79$. Because

$$5 < 64 - 57.65 - 0.79$$

the condition in equation (10.8) is violated. An arbitrageur should buy the option and short the stock. This generates 64 – 5 = $59. The arbitrageur invests $0.79 of this at 12% for one month to pay the dividend of $0.80 in one month. The remaining $58.21 is invested for four months at 12%. Regardless of what happens a profit will materialize.
If the stock price declines below $60 in four months, the arbitrageur loses the $5 spent on the option but gains on the short position. The arbitrageur shorts when the stock price is $64, has to pay dividends with a present value of $0.79, and closes out the short position when the stock price is $60 or less. Because $57.65 is the present value of $60, the short position generates at

least $64 - 57.65 - 0.79 = \$5.56$ in present value terms. The present value of the arbitrageur's gain is therefore at least $5.56 - 5.00 = \$0.56$.

If the stock price is above $60 at the expiration of the option, the option is exercised. The arbitrageur buys the stock for $60 in four months and closes out the short position. The present value of the $60 paid for the stock is $57.65 and as before the dividend has a present value of $0.79. The gain from the short position and the exercise of the option is therefore exactly $64 - 57.65 - 0.79 = \$5.56$. The arbitrageur's gain in present value terms is $5.56 - 5.00 = \$0.56$.

Problem 10.12.

A one-month European put option on a non-dividend-paying stock is currently selling for $2.50. The stock price is $47, the strike price is $50, and the risk-free interest rate is 6% per annum. What opportunities are there for an arbitrageur?

In this case the present value of the strike price is $50e^{-0.06 \times 1/12} = 49.75$. Because
$$2.5 < 49.75 - 47.00$$
the condition in equation (10.5) is violated. An arbitrageur should borrow $49.50 at 6% for one month, buy the stock, and buy the put option. This generates a profit in all circumstances.

If the stock price is above $50 in one month, the option expires worthless, but the stock can be sold for at least $50. A sum of $50 received in one month has a present value of $49.75 today. The strategy therefore generates profit with a present value of at least $0.25.

If the stock price is below $50 in one month the put option is exercised and the stock owned is sold for exactly $50 (or $49.75 in present value terms). The trading strategy therefore generates a profit of exactly $0.25 in present value terms.

Problem 10.13.

Give an intuitive explanation of why the early exercise of an American put becomes more attractive as the risk-free rate increases and volatility decreases.

The early exercise of an American put is attractive when the interest earned on the strike price is greater than the insurance element lost. When interest rates increase, the value of the interest earned on the strike price increases making early exercise more attractive. When volatility decreases, the insurance element is less valuable. Again, this makes early exercise more attractive.

Problem 10.14.

The price of a European call that expires in six months and has a strike price of $30 is $2. The underlying stock price is $29, and a dividend of $0.50 is expected in two months and again in five months. Risk-free interest rates for all maturities are 10%. What is the price of a European put option that expires in six months and has a strike price of $30?

Using the notation in the chapter, put-call parity, equation (10.10), gives
$$c + Ke^{-rT} + D = p + S_0$$
or
$$p = c + Ke^{-rT} + D - S_0$$
In this case

$$p = 2 + 30e^{-0.1 \times 6/12} + (0.5e^{-0.1 \times 2/12} + 0.5e^{-0.1 \times 5/12}) - 29 = 2.51$$

In other words the put price is $2.51.

Problem 10.15.
Explain carefully the arbitrage opportunities in Problem 10.14 if the European put price is $3.

If the put price is $3.00, it is too high relative to the call price. An arbitrageur should buy the call, short the put and short the stock. This generates $-2 + 3 + 29 = \$30$ in cash which is invested at 10%. Regardless of what happens a profit with a present value of $3.00 - 2.51 = \$0.49$ is locked in.

If the stock price is above $30 in six months, the call option is exercised, and the put option expires worthless. The call option enables the stock to be bought for $30, or $30e^{-0.10 \times 6/12} = \$28.54$ in present value terms. The dividends on the short position cost $0.5e^{-0.1 \times 2/12} + 0.5e^{-0.1 \times 5/12} = \$0.97$ in present value terms so that there is a profit with a present value of $30 - 28.54 - 0.97 = \$0.49$.

If the stock price is below $30 in six months, the put option is exercised and the call option expires worthless. The short put option leads to the stock being bought for $30, or $30e^{-0.10 \times 6/12} = \$28.54$ in present value terms. The dividends on the short position cost $0.5e^{-0.1 \times 2/12} + 0.5e^{-0.1 \times 5/12} = \$0.97$ in present value terms so that there is a profit with a present value of $30 - 28.54 - 0.97 = \$0.49$.

Problem 10.16.
The price of an American call on a non-dividend-paying stock is $4. The stock price is $31, the strike price is $30, and the expiration date is in three months. The risk-free interest rate is 8%. Derive upper and lower bounds for the price of an American put on the same stock with the same strike price and expiration date.

From equation (10.7)

$$S_0 - K \leq C - P \leq S_0 - Ke^{-rT}$$

In this case

$$31 - 30 \leq 4 - P \leq 31 - 30e^{-0.08 \times 0.25}$$

or

$$1.00 \leq 4.00 - P \leq 1.59$$

or

$$2.41 \leq P \leq 3.00$$

Upper and lower bounds for the price of an American put are therefore $2.41 and $3.00.

Problem 10.17.
Explain carefully the arbitrage opportunities in Problem 10.16 if the American put price is greater than the calculated upper bound.

If the American put price is greater than $3.00 an arbitrageur can sell the American put, short the stock, and buy the American call. This realizes at least $3 + 31 - 4 = \$30$ which can be invested at the risk-free interest rate. At some stage during the 3-month period either the American put or the American call will be exercised. The arbitrageur then pays $30, receives the stock and closes out the short position. The cash flows to the arbitrageur are +$30 at time zero and −$30 at some future time. These cash flows have a positive present value.

Problem 10.18.
Prove the result in equation (10.7). (Hint: For the first part of the relationship consider (a) a portfolio consisting of a European call plus an amount of cash equal to K and (b) a portfolio consisting of an American put option plus one share.)

As in the text we use c and p to denote the European call and put option price, and C and P to denote the American call and put option prices. Because $P \geq p$, it follows from put–call parity that

$$P \geq c + Ke^{-rT} - S_0$$

and since $c = C$,

$$P \geq C + Ke^{-rT} - S_0$$

or

$$C - P \leq S_0 - Ke^{-rT}$$

For a further relationship between C and P, consider
Portfolio I: One European call option plus an amount of cash equal to K.
Portfolio J: One American put option plus one share.

Both options have the same exercise price and expiration date. Assume that the cash in portfolio I is invested at the risk-free interest rate. If the put option is not exercised early portfolio J is worth

$$\max(S_T, K)$$

at time T. Portfolio I is worth

$$\max(S_T - K, 0) + Ke^{rT} = \max(S_T, K) - K + Ke^{rT}$$

at this time. Portfolio I is therefore worth more than portfolio J. Suppose next that the put option in portfolio J is exercised early, say, at time τ. This means that portfolio J is worth K at time τ. However, even if the call option were worthless, portfolio I would be worth $Ke^{r\tau}$ at time τ. It follows that portfolio I is worth at least as much as portfolio J in all circumstances. Hence

$$c + K \geq P + S_0$$

Since $c = C$,

$$C + K \geq P + S_0$$

or

$$C - P \geq S_0 - K$$

Combining this with the other inequality derived above for $C - P$, we obtain

$$S_0 - K \leq C - P \leq S_0 - Ke^{-rT}$$

Problem 10.19.
Prove the result in equation (10.11). (Hint: For the first part of the relationship consider (a) a portfolio consisting of a European call plus an amount of cash equal to $D + K$ and (b) a

portfolio consisting of an American put option plus one share.)

As in the text we use c and p to denote the European call and put option price, and C and P to denote the American call and put option prices. The present value of the dividends will be denoted by D. As shown in the answer to Problem 10.18, when there are no dividends

$$C - P \leq S_0 - Ke^{-rT}$$

Dividends reduce C and increase P. Hence this relationship must also be true when there are dividends.

For a further relationship between C and P, consider

Portfolio I: one European call option plus an amount of cash equal to $D + K$

Portfolio J: one American put option plus one share

Both options have the same exercise price and expiration date. Assume that the cash in portfolio I is invested at the risk-free interest rate. If the put option is not exercised early, portfolio J is worth

$$\max(S_T, K) + De^{rT}$$

at time T. Portfolio I is worth

$$\max(S_T - K, 0) + (D + K)e^{rT} = \max(S_T, K) + De^{rT} + Ke^{rT} - K$$

at this time. Portfolio I is therefore worth more than portfolio J. Suppose next that the put option in portfolio J is exercised early, say, at time τ. This means that portfolio J is worth at most $K + De^{r\tau}$ at time τ. However, even if the call option were worthless, portfolio I would be worth $(D + K)e^{r\tau}$ at time τ. It follows that portfolio I is worth more than portfolio J in all circumstances. Hence

$$c + D + K \geq P + S_0$$

Because $C \geq c$

$$C - P \geq S_0 - D - K$$

Problem 10.20.

Consider a five-year call option on a non-dividend-paying stock granted to employees. The option can be exercised at any time after the end of the first year. Unlike a regular exchange-traded call option, the employee stock option cannot be sold. What is the likely impact of this restriction on early exercise?

An employee stock option may be exercised early because the employee needs cash or because he or she is uncertain about the company's future prospects. Regular call options can be sold in the market in either of these two situations, but employee stock options cannot be sold. In theory an employee can short the company's stock as an alternative to exercising. In practice this is not usually encouraged and may even be illegal for senior managers. These points are discussed further in Chapter 14.

Problem 10.21.

Use the software DerivaGem to verify that Figures 10.1 and 10.2 are correct.

The graphs can be produced from the first worksheet in DerivaGem. Select Equity as the

Underlying Type. Select Analytic European as the Option Type. Input stock price as 50, volatility as 30%, risk-free rate as 5%, time to exercise as 1 year, and exercise price as 50. Leave the dividend table blank because we are assuming no dividends. Select the button corresponding to call. Do not select the implied volatility button. Hit the *Enter* key and click on calculate. DerivaGem will show the price of the option as 7.15562248. Move to the Graph Results on the right hand side of the worksheet. Enter Option Price for the vertical axis and Asset price for the horizontal axis. Choose the minimum strike price value as 10 (software will not accept 0) and the maximum strike price value as 100. Hit *Enter* and click on *Draw Graph*. This will produce Figure 10.1a. Figures 10.1c, 10.1e, 10.2a, and 10.2c can be produced similarly by changing the horizontal axis. By selecting put instead of call and recalculating the rest of the figures can be produced. You are encouraged to experiment with this worksheet. Try different parameter values and different types of options.

Problem 10.22.

What is the impact (if any) of negative interest rates on:
  a) *The put–call parity result for European options*
  b) *The result that American call options on non-dividend-paying stocks should never be exercised early.*
  c) *The result that American put options on non-dividend paying stocks should sometimes be exercised early.*
Assume that holding cash earning zero interest is not possible.

  a) The put-call parity result still holds. The arguments are unchanged.
  b) Deep-in-the-money American calls might be exercised early because option holder will prefer to pay the strike price earlier.
  c) Deep-in the-money American puts should not be exercised early because the holder would rather delay receiving the strike price.

CHAPTER 11
Trading Strategies Involving Options

This is a fun chapter that should not cause you too many problems. It describes some of the ways options can be used to produce interesting profit patterns. The chapter starts by considering principal-protected notes. These are retail products structured in such a way that the investor can take a position on future movements in a particular market variable without risking his or her principal. It then moves on to consider ways in which option positions can be combined with each other and with positions in the underlying asset.

Figure 11.1 shows what can be achieved by taking a position in the option and the underlying asset. As put-call parity shows, a long or short position in the underlying asset can be used to convert a) a short put to something that looks like a short call, b) a long call to something that looks like a long put, c) a long put to something that looks like a long call, and d) a short put to something that looks like a short call.

Spread is the word used to describe a position in two or more calls or two or more puts. Put-call parity shows that a spread created using calls can also be created using puts. This is shown for four types of spreads in the chapter: bull spreads (see Figures 11.2 and 11.3); bear spreads (see Figures 11.4 and 11.5); butterfly spreads (see Figures 11.6 and 11.7); and calendar spreads (see Figures 11.8 and 11.9).

Combination is the word used to describe a position involving both calls and puts. A straddle involves buying a call and a put with the same strike price and maturity date. A strangle involves buying a call and a put when the strike price of the call is greater than that of the put.

In theory any payoff pattern can be created by using calls and puts with different strike prices in an appropriate way. Figure 11.13 shows that a butterfly spread can be used to create a payoff pattern that is a small "spike." Any specified payoff pattern can be created by combining spikes judiciously.

Answers to Practice Questions

Problem 11.8.
Use put–call parity to relate the initial investment for a bull spread created using calls to the initial investment for a bull spread created using puts.

A bull spread using calls provides a profit pattern with the same general shape as a bull spread using puts (see Figures 11.2 and 11.3 in the text). Define p_1 and c_1 as the prices of put and call with strike price K_1 and p_2 and c_2 as the prices of a put and call with strike price K_2. From put-call parity

$$p_1 + S = c_1 + K_1 e^{-rT}$$

66

$$p_2 + S = c_2 + K_2 e^{-rT}$$

Hence:

$$p_1 - p_2 = c_1 - c_2 - (K_2 - K_1)e^{-rT}$$

This shows that the initial investment when the spread is created from puts is less than the initial investment when it is created from calls by an amount $(K_2 - K_1)e^{-rT}$. In fact as mentioned in the text the initial investment when the bull spread is created from puts is negative, while the initial investment when it is created from calls is positive.

The profit when calls are used to create the bull spread is higher than when puts are used by $(K_2 - K_1)(1 - e^{-rT})$. This reflects the fact that the call strategy involves an additional risk-free investment of $(K_2 - K_1)e^{-rT}$ over the put strategy. This earns interest of

$$(K_2 - K_1)e^{-rT}(e^{rT} - 1) = (K_2 - K_1)(1 - e^{-rT}).$$

Problem 11.9.
Explain how an aggressive bear spread can be created using put options.

An aggressive bull spread using call options is discussed in the text. Both of the options used have relatively high strike prices. Similarly, an aggressive bear spread can be created using put options. Both of the options should be out of the money (that is, they should have relatively low strike prices). The spread then costs very little to set up because both of the puts are worth close to zero. In most circumstances the spread will provide zero payoff. However, there is a small chance that the stock price will fall fast so that on expiration both options will be in the money. The spread then provides a payoff equal to the difference between the two strike prices, $K_2 - K_1$.

Problem 11.10.
Suppose that put options on a stock with strike prices $30 and $35 cost $4 and $7, respectively. How can the options be used to create (a) a bull spread and (b) a bear spread? Construct a table that shows the profit and payoff for both spreads.

A bull spread is created by buying the $30 put and selling the $35 put. This strategy gives rise to an initial cash inflow of $3. The outcome is as follows:

Stock Price	Payoff	Profit
$S_T \geq 35$	0	3
$30 \leq S_T < 35$	$S_T - 35$	$S_T - 32$
$S_T < 30$	-5	-2

A bear spread is created by selling the $30 put and buying the $35 put. This strategy costs $3 initially. The outcome is as follows

67

Stock Price	Payoff	Profit
$S_T \geq 35$	0	-3
$30 \leq S_T < 35$	$35 - S_T$	$32 - S_T$
$S_T < 30$	5	2

Problem 11.11.

Use put–call parity to show that the cost of a butterfly spread created from European puts is identical to the cost of a butterfly spread created from European calls.

Define c_1, c_2, and c_3 as the prices of calls with strike prices K_1, K_2 and K_3. Define p_1, p_2 and p_3 as the prices of puts with strike prices K_1, K_2 and K_3. With the usual notation

$$c_1 + K_1 e^{-rT} = p_1 + S$$

$$c_2 + K_2 e^{-rT} = p_2 + S$$

$$c_3 + K_3 e^{-rT} = p_3 + S$$

Hence

$$c_1 + c_3 - 2c_2 + (K_1 + K_3 - 2K_2)e^{-rT} = p_1 + p_3 - 2p_2$$

Because $K_2 - K_1 = K_3 - K_2$, it follows that $K_1 + K_3 - 2K_2 = 0$ and

$$c_1 + c_3 - 2c_2 = p_1 + p_3 - 2p_2$$

The cost of a butterfly spread created using European calls is therefore exactly the same as the cost of a butterfly spread created using European puts.

Problem 11.12.

A call with a strike price of $60 costs $6. A put with the same strike price and expiration date costs $4. Construct a table that shows the profit from a straddle. For what range of stock prices would the straddle lead to a loss?

A straddle is created by buying both the call and the put. This strategy costs $10. The profit/loss is shown in the following table:

Stock Price	Payoff	Profit
$S_T > 60$	$S_T - 60$	$S_T - 70$
$S_T \leq 60$	$60 - S_T$	$50 - S_T$

This shows that the straddle will lead to a loss if the final stock price is between $50 and $70.

Problem 11.13.

Construct a table showing the payoff from a bull spread when puts with strike prices K_1 and K_2 are used $(K_2 > K_1)$.

The bull spread is created by buying a put with strike price K_1 and selling a put with strike price K_2. The payoff is calculated as follows:

Stock Price	Payoff from Long Put	Payoff from Short Put	Total Payoff
$S_T \geq K_2$	0	0	0
$K_1 < S_T < K_2$	0	$S_T - K_2$	$-(K_2 - S_T)$
$S_T \leq K_1$	$K_1 - S_T$	$S_T - K_2$	$-(K_2 - K_1)$

Problem 11.14.
An investor believes that there will be a big jump in a stock price, but is uncertain as to the direction. Identify six different strategies the investor can follow and explain the differences among them.

Possible strategies are:

  Strangle
  Straddle
  Strip
  Strap
  Reverse calendar spread
  Reverse butterfly spread

The strategies all provide positive profits when there are large stock price moves. A strangle is less expensive than a straddle, but requires a bigger move in the stock price in order to provide a positive profit. Strips and straps are more expensive than straddles but provide bigger profits in certain circumstances. A strip will provide a bigger profit when there is a large downward stock price move. A strap will provide a bigger profit when there is a large upward stock price move. In the case of strangles, straddles, strips and straps, the profit increases as the size of the stock price movement increases. By contrast in a reverse calendar spread and a reverse butterfly spread there is a maximum potential profit regardless of the size of the stock price movement.

Problem 11.15.
How can a forward contract on a stock with a particular delivery price and delivery date be created from options?

Suppose that the delivery price is K and the delivery date is T. The forward contract is created by buying a European call and selling a European put when both options have strike price K and exercise date T. This portfolio provides a payoff of $S_T - K$ under all circumstances where S_T is the stock price at time T. Suppose that F_0 is the forward price. If $K = F_0$, the forward contract that is created has zero value. This shows that the price of a call equals the price of a put when the strike price is F_0.

Problem 11.16.

"A box spread comprises four options. Two can be combined to create a long forward position and two can be combined to create a short forward position." Explain this statement.

A box spread is a bull spread created using calls together with a bear spread created using puts. With the notation in the text it consists of a) a long call with strike K_1, b) a short call with strike K_2, c) a long put with strike K_2, and d) a short put with strike K_1. a) and d) give a long forward contract with delivery price K_1; b) and c) give a short forward contract with delivery price K_2. The two forward contracts taken together give the payoff of $K_2 - K_1$.

Problem 11.17.

What is the result if the strike price of the put is higher than the strike price of the call in a strangle?

The result is shown in Figure S11.1. The profit pattern from a long position in a call and a put is much the same when a) the put has a higher strike price than a call and b) when the call has a higher strike price than the put. But both the initial investment and the final payoff are much higher in the first case.

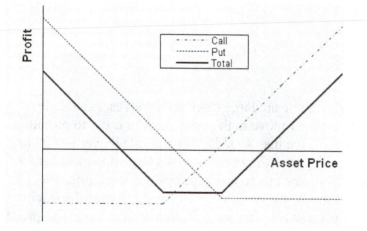

Figure S11.1   Profit Pattern in Problem 11.17

Problem 11.18.

A foreign currency is currently worth $0.64. A one-year butterfly spread is set up using European call options with strike prices of $0.60, $0.65, and $0.70. The risk-free interest rates in the United States and the foreign country are 5% and 4% respectively, and the volatility of the exchange rate is 15%. Use the DerivaGem software to calculate the cost of setting up the butterfly spread position. Show that the cost is the same if European put options are used instead of European call options.

To use DerivaGem select the first worksheet in DG400f.xls and choose Currency as the Underlying Type. Select Black-Scholes European as the Option Type. Input exchange rate as

0.64, volatility as 15%, risk-free rate as 5%, foreign risk-free interest rate as 4%, time to exercise as 1 year, and exercise price as 0.60. Select the button corresponding to call. Do not select the implied volatility button. Hit the *Enter* key and click on calculate. DerivaGem will show the price of the option as 0.0618. Change the exercise price to 0.65, hit *Enter*, and click on calculate again. DerivaGem will show the value of the option as 0.0352. Change the exercise price to 0.70, hit *Enter*, and click on *Calculate*. DerivaGem will show the value of the option as 0.0181. Now select the button corresponding to put and repeat the procedure. DerivaGem shows the values of puts with strike prices 0.60, 0.65, and 0.70 to be 0.0176, 0.0386, and 0.0690, respectively.

The cost of setting up the butterfly spread when calls are used is therefore
$$0.0618 + 0.0181 - 2 \times 0.0352 = 0.0095$$
The cost of setting up the butterfly spread when puts are used is
$$0.0176 + 0.0690 - 2 \times 0.0386 = 0.0094$$
Allowing for rounding errors, these two are the same.

Problem 11.19
An index provides a dividend yield of 1% and has a volatility of 20%. The risk-free interest rate is 4%. How long does a principal-protected note, created as in Example 11.1, have to last for it to be profitable for the bank issuing it? Use DerivaGem.

Assume that the investment in the index is initially $100. (This is a scaling factor that makes no difference to the result.) DerivaGem can be used to value an option on the index with the index level equal to 100, the volatility equal to 20%, the risk-free rate equal to 4%, the dividend yield equal to 1%, and the exercise price equal to 100. For different times to maturity, T, we value a call option (using Black-Scholes European) and calculate the funds available to buy the call option ($=100-100e^{-0.04 \times T}$). Results are as follows:

Time to maturity, T	Funds Available	Value of Option
1	3.92	9.32
2	7.69	13.79
5	18.13	23.14
10	32.97	33.34
11	35.60	34.91

This table shows that the answer is between 10 and 11 years. Continuing the calculations we find that if the life of the principal-protected note is 10.35 year or more, it is profitable for the bank. (Excel's Solver can be used in conjunction with the DerivaGem functions to facilitate calculations.)

CHAPTER 12
Introduction to Binomial Trees

This chapter introduces binomial trees. There are a number of reasons why binomial trees are covered at this relatively early stage in the book:

1. Binomial trees illustrate the no-arbitrage arguments that can be used to derive the Black-Scholes-Merton model
2. Binomial trees illustrate the delta hedging strategies that can be used to hedge a position in an option with a position in the underlying asset
3. Binomial trees illustrate the risk-neutral valuation argument. This is of central importance in the pricing of derivatives
4. Binomial trees constitute an important numerical procedure for valuing American options. (The material in this chapter is extended in Chapter 18)

The chapter starts by considering one-step binomial trees for call options on a stock (see, for example, Figure 12.1). The option lasts until time T and there are assumed to be only two possible stock prices at time T and therefore only two possible option prices. We consider portfolios consisting of a short position in one call option and a long position in Δ (delta) shares of the stock. For some value of Δ the portfolio has the same value for both of the possible final stock prices. We determine this value of Δ (see equation 12.1). For this value of Δ the portfolio is riskless because its payoff at time T is known for certain. As such it must earn the risk-free rate. The value of the portfolio today is the present value of the portfolio at time T. The value of the stock price is known today. The option price can therefore be calculated. (See equations 12.2 and 12.3.)

Section 12.2 shows that in the case of a one-step binomial tree the option can be valued by
1. Assuming that the expected return on the stock is the risk-free rate; and
2. Discounting the expected payoff on the option at the risk-free rate.

This is the risk-neutral valuation argument. It is a very important argument in option pricing. It says that if we assume that all market participants are risk-neutral (in the sense that they require the risk-free rate as the expected return on all risky assets) then we get the right price for options. The price is not just correct in a risk-neutral world. It is correct in all other worlds as well.

Section 12.3 covers two-step binomial trees. In these, the life of the option is divided into two equal time steps. The change in the stock price during each time step is assumed to be given by a one-step binomial tree (with the proportional up- and down-movements being the same). This means that there are three possible final stock prices. (See for example Figure 12.3.) Evaluating the price of the option involves working back through the tree applying the risk-neutral analysis given in Section 12.2. The procedure for evaluating a put option is analogous to the procedure for valuing a call option. If the option is American we test whether early exercise is optimal at each node of the tree by calculating the value of the option with and without early exercise and taking the greater of the two. You should compare Figures 12.7 and 12.8 and make sure you understand the difference. They are being used to value the same option except that in Figure 12.7 the option is European whereas in Figure 12.8 it is American.

Once you have mastered two-step trees it is not difficult to extend the ideas in the chapter to multistep trees. Section 12.7 gives formulas for calculating the proportional up movement, u, the proportional down movement, d, and the risk-neutral probability of an up movement, p, from the stock price volatility, σ, the length of the time step, Δt, and the risk-free rate, r. The formulas are:

$$u = e^{\sigma\sqrt{\Delta t}}$$

$$d = \frac{1}{u}$$

$$p = \frac{a - d}{u - d}$$

where

$$a = e^{r\Delta t}$$

The last part of the chapter looks ahead to later chapters and explains how the binomial tree methodology can be used to value call and put options on stock indices, currencies, and futures contracts. The formulas are the same as those given above except that

$$a = e^{(r-q)\Delta t}$$

where

1. In the case of an option on a stock index, q is the average dividend yield on the index during the life of the option.
2. In the case of an option on a foreign currency, q is the foreign risk-free rate.
3. In the case of an option on a futures contract, $q = r$ so that $a = 1$.

Software

If you have not already done so, this would be a good time to start using the Equity_FX_Indx_Fut_Calc worksheet of DG400f.xls. Choose as the Option Type *Binomial: European* or *Binomial American* and indicate in *Tree Steps* the number of steps you want to use on the tree. Once you have calculated the price of an option you can click on a box to display the tree and see the calculations that have been carried out. If you specify more than 10 tree steps the tree displayed is the one that would be used if 10 tree steps had been specified.

Answers to Practice Questions

Problem 12.8.
Consider the situation in which stock price movements during the life of a European option are governed by a two-step binomial tree. Explain why it is not possible to set up a position in the stock and the option that remains riskless for the whole of the life of the option.

The riskless portfolio consists of a short position in the option and a long position in Δ shares. Because Δ changes during the life of the option, this riskless portfolio must also change.

Problem 12.9.

A stock price is currently $50. It is known that at the end of two months it will be either $53 or $48. The risk-free interest rate is 10% per annum with continuous compounding. What is the value of a two-month European call option with a strikeprice of $49? Use no-arbitrage arguments.

At the end of two months the value of the option will be either $4 (if the stock price is $53) or $0 (if the stock price is $48). Consider a portfolio consisting of:

$$+\Delta \quad : \quad \text{shares}$$
$$-1 \quad : \quad \text{option}$$

The value of the portfolio is either 48Δ or $53\Delta - 4$ in two months. If
$$48\Delta = 53\Delta - 4$$
i.e.,
$$\Delta = 0.8$$
the value of the portfolio is certain to be 38.4. For this value of Δ the portfolio is therefore riskless. The current value of the portfolio is:
$$0.8 \times 50 - f$$
where f is the value of the option. Since the portfolio must earn the risk-free rate of interest
$$(0.8 \times 50 - f)e^{0.10 \times 2/12} = 38.4$$
i.e.,
$$f = 2.23$$
The value of the option is therefore $2.23.

This can also be calculated directly from equations (12.2) and (12.3). $u = 1.06$, $d = 0.96$ so that
$$p = \frac{e^{0.10 \times 2/12} - 0.96}{1.06 - 0.96} = 0.5681$$
and
$$f = e^{-0.10 \times 2/12} \times 0.5681 \times 4 = 2.23$$

Problem 12.10.

A stock price is currently $80. It is known that at the end of four months it will be either $75 or $85. The risk-free interest rate is 5% per annum with continuous compounding. What is the value of a four-month European put option with a strike price of $80? Use no-arbitrage arguments.

At the end of four months the value of the option will be either $5 (if the stock price is $75) or $0 (if the stock price is $85). Consider a portfolio consisting of:

$$-\Delta \quad : \quad \text{shares}$$
$$+1 \quad : \quad \text{option}$$

(Note: The delta, Δ of a put option is negative. We have constructed the portfolio so that it is +1 option and $-\Delta$ shares rather than -1 option and $+\Delta$ shares so that the initial investment is positive.)

74

The value of the portfolio is either -85Δ or $-75\Delta+5$ in four months. If
$$-85\Delta=-75\Delta+5$$
i.e.,
$$\Delta=-0.5$$
the value of the portfolio is certain to be 42.5. For this value of Δ the portfolio is therefore riskless. The current value of the portfolio is:
$$0.5\times80+f$$
where f is the value of the option. Since the portfolio is riskless
$$(0.5\times80+f)e^{0.05\times4/12}=42.5$$
i.e.,
$$f=1.80$$
The value of the option is therefore $1.80.
This can also be calculated directly from equations (12.2) and (12.3). $u=1.0625$, $d=0.9375$ so that
$$p=\frac{e^{0.05\times4/12}-0.9375}{1.0625-0.9375}=0.6345$$
$1-p=0.3655$ and
$$f=e^{-0.05\times4/12}\times0.3655\times5=1.80$$

Problem 12.11.

A stock price is currently $40. It is known that at the end of three months it will be either $45 or $35. The risk-free rate of interest with quarterly compounding is 8% per annum. Calculate the value of a three-month European put option on the stock with an exercise price of $40. Verify that no-arbitrage arguments and risk-neutral valuation arguments give the same answers.

At the end of three months the value of the option is either $5 (if the stock price is $35) or $0 (if the stock price is $45).
Consider a portfolio consisting of:
$$-\Delta\quad:\quad\text{shares}$$
$$+1\quad:\quad\text{option}$$
(Note: The delta, Δ, of a put option is negative. We have constructed the portfolio so that it is $+1$ option and $-\Delta$ shares rather than -1 option and $+\Delta$ shares so that the initial investment is positive.)
The value of the portfolio is either $-35\Delta+5$ or -45Δ. If:
$$-35\Delta+5=-45\Delta$$
i.e.,
$$\Delta=-0.5$$
the value of the portfolio is certain to be 22.5. For this value of Δ the portfolio is therefore riskless. The current value of the portfolio is
$$-40\Delta+f$$
where f is the value of the option. Since the portfolio must earn the risk-free rate of interest
$$(40\times0.5+f)\times1.02=22.5$$
Hence

$$f = 2.06$$

i.e., the value of the option is $2.06.

This can also be calculated using risk-neutral valuation. Suppose that p is the probability of an upward stock price movement in a risk-neutral world. We must have

$$45p + 35(1-p) = 40 \times 1.02$$

i.e.,

$$10p = 5.8$$

or:

$$p = 0.58$$

The expected value of the option in a risk-neutral world is:

$$0 \times 0.58 + 5 \times 0.42 = 2.10$$

This has a present value of

$$\frac{2.10}{1.02} = 2.06$$

This is consistent with the no-arbitrage answer.

Problem 12.12.

A stock price is currently $50. Over each of the next two three-month periods it is expected to go up by 6% or down by 5%. The risk-free interest rate is 5% per annum with continuous compounding. What is the value of a six-month European call option with a strike price of $51?

A tree describing the behavior of the stock price is shown in Figure S12.1. The risk-neutral probability of an up move, p, is given by

$$p = \frac{e^{0.05 \times 3/12} - 0.95}{1.06 - 0.95} = 0.5689$$

There is a payoff from the option of $56.18 - 51 = 5.18$ for the highest final node (which corresponds to two up moves) zero in all other cases. The value of the option is therefore

$$5.18 \times 0.5689^2 \times e^{-0.05 \times 6/12} = 1.635$$

This can also be calculated by working back through the tree as indicated in Figure S12.1. The value of the call option is the lower number at each node in the figure.

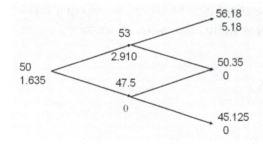

Figure S12.1 Tree for Problem 12.12

Problem 12.13.

For the situation considered in Problem 12.12, what is the value of a six-month European put option with a strike price of $51? Verify that the European call and European put prices satisfy *put–call parity. If the put option were American, would it ever be optimal to exercise it early at any of the nodes on the tree?*

The tree for valuing the put option is shown in Figure S12.2. We get a payoff of $51-50.35 = 0.65$ if the middle final node is reached and a payoff of $51-45.125 = 5.875$ if the lowest final node is reached. The value of the option is therefore
$$(0.65\times2\times0.5689\times0.4311+5.875\times0.4311^2)e^{-0.05\times6/12} = 1.376$$
This can also be calculated by working back through the tree as indicated in Figure S12.2. The value of the put plus the stock price is from Problem 12.12
$$1.376+50 = 51.376$$
The value of the call plus the present value of the strike price is
$$1.635+51e^{-0.05\times6/12} = 51.376$$
This verifies that put–call parity holds
To test whether it worth exercising the option early we compare the value calculated for the option at each node with the payoff from immediate exercise. At node C the payoff from immediate exercise is $51-47.5 = 3.5$. Because this is greater than 2.8664, the option should be exercised at this node. The option should not be exercised at either node A or node B.

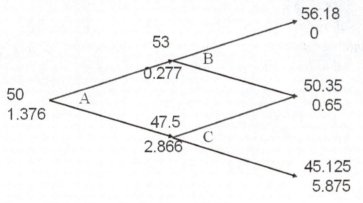

Figure S12.2 Tree for Problem 12.13

Problem 12.14.

A stock price is currently $25. It is known that at the end of two months it will be either $23 or $27. The risk-free interest rate is 10% per annum with continuous compounding. Suppose S_T is the stock price at the end of two months. What is the value of a derivative that pays off S_T^2 at this time?

This problem shows that the valuation procedures introduced in the chapter can be used for derivatives other than call and put options.
At the end of two months the value of the derivative will be either 529 (if the stock price is 23) or 729 (if the stock price is 27). Consider a portfolio consisting of:

$$+\Delta \quad : \quad \text{shares}$$
$$-1 \quad : \quad \text{derivative}$$

The value of the portfolio is either $27\Delta-729$ or $23\Delta-529$ in two months. If

$$27\Delta - 729 = 23\Delta - 529$$

i.e.,

$$\Delta = 50$$

the value of the portfolio is certain to be 621. For this value of Δ the portfolio is therefore riskless. The current value of the portfolio is:

$$50 \times 25 - f$$

where f is the value of the derivative. Since the portfolio must earn the risk-free rate of interest

$$(50 \times 25 - f)e^{0.10 \times 2/12} = 621$$

i.e.,

$$f = 639.3$$

The value of the option is therefore \$639.3.

This can also be calculated directly from equations (12.2) and (12.3). $u = 1.08$, $d = 0.92$ so that

$$p = \frac{e^{0.10 \times 2/12} - 0.92}{1.08 - 0.92} = 0.6050$$

and

$$f = e^{-0.10 \times 2/12}(0.6050 \times 729 + 0.3950 \times 529) = 639.3$$

Problem 12.15.

Calculate u, d, and p when a binomial tree is constructed to value an option on a foreign currency. The tree step size is one month, the domestic interest rate is 5% per annum, the foreign interest rate is 8% per annum, and the volatility is 12% per annum.

In this case

$$a = e^{(0.05-0.08) \times 1/12} = 0.9975$$

$$u = e^{0.12\sqrt{1/12}} = 1.0352$$

$$d = 1/u = 0.9660$$

$$p = \frac{0.9975 - 0.9660}{1.0352 - 0.9660} = 0.4553$$

Problem 12.16.

The volatility of a non-dividend-paying stock whose price is \$78, is 30%. The risk-free rate is 3% per annum (continuously compounded) for all maturities. Calculate values for u, d, and p when a two-month time step is used. What is the value of a four-month European call option with a strike price of \$80 given by a two-step binomial tree. Suppose a trader sells 1,000 options (10 contracts). What position in the stock is necessary to hedge the trader's position at the time of the trade?

$$u = e^{0.30\times\sqrt{0.1667}} = 1.1303$$
$$d = 1/u = 0.8847$$
$$p = \frac{e^{0.30\times2/12} - 0.8847}{1.1303 - 0.8847} = 0.4898$$

The tree is given in Figure S12.3. The value of the option is $4.67. The initial delta is 9.58/(88.16 – 69.01) which is almost exactly 0.5 so that 500 shares should be purchased.

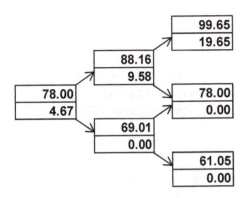

| 99.65 |
| 19.65 |

| 88.16 |
| 9.58 |

| 78.00 |
| 4.67 |

| 78.00 |
| 0.00 |

| 69.01 |
| 0.00 |

| 61.05 |
| 0.00 |

Figure S12.3: Tree for Problem 12.16

Problem 12.17.
A stock index is currently 1,500. Its volatility is 18%. The risk-free rate is 4% per annum (continuously compounded) for all maturities and the dividend yield on the index is 2.5%. Calculate values for u, d, and p when a six-month time step is used. What is the value a 12-month American put option with a strike price of 1,480 given by a two-step binomial tree.

$$u = e^{0.18\times\sqrt{0.5}} = 1.1357$$
$$d = 1/u = 0.8805$$
$$p = \frac{e^{(0.04-0.025)\times0.5} - 0.8805}{1.1357 - 0.8805} = 0.4977$$

The tree is shown in Figure S12.4. The option is exercised at the lower node at the six-month point. It is worth 78.41.

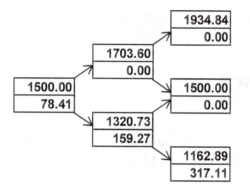

Figure S12.4: Tree for Problem 12.17

Problem 12.18

The futures price of a commodity is $90. Use a three-step tree to value (a) a nine-month American call option with strike price $93 and (b) a nine-month American put option with strike price $93. The volatility is 28% and the risk-free rate (all maturities) is 3% with continuous compounding.

$$u = e^{0.28 \times \sqrt{0.25}} = 1.1503$$

$$d = 1/u = 0.8694$$

$$u = \frac{1 - 0.8694}{1.1503 - 0.8694} = 0.4651$$

The tree for valuing the call is in Figure S12.5a and that for valuing the put is in Figure S12.5b. The values are 7.94 and 10.88, respectively.

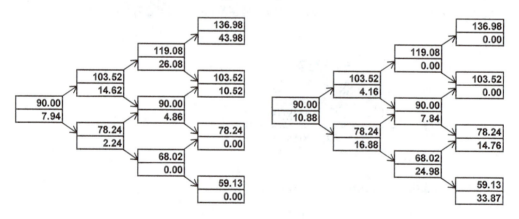

Figure S12.5a: Call   **Figure S12.5b:** Put

CHAPTER 13
Valuing Stock Options: The Black-Scholes-Merton Model

This is the point at which the book begins to get a little more technical! Chapter 13 presents the path-breaking stock option pricing model published by Fischer Black, Myron Scholes, and Robert Merton in 1973. The Black-Scholes-Merton model is based on the assumption that the stock price at any future time has a lognormal probability distribution (see Figure 13.1). This assumption is valid in a world where the return on the stock follows a random walk.

The Black-Scholes-Merton model is given by equations (13.5) and (13.6):

$$c = S_0 N(d_1) - Ke^{-rT} N(d_2)$$

$$p = Ke^{-rT} N(-d_2) - S_0 N(-d_1)$$

where

$$d_1 = \frac{\ln(S_0/K) + (r + \sigma^2/2)T}{\sigma\sqrt{T}}$$

$$d_2 = \frac{\ln(S_0/K) + (r - \sigma^2/2)T}{\sigma\sqrt{T}} = d_1 - \sigma\sqrt{T}$$

In these equations, c and p are the prices of European call and put options on the stock, S_0 is the current stock price, K is the strike price, r is the risk-free rate, σ is the volatility, and T is the time to maturity. The function $N(x)$ is the cumulative probability distribution function for a normally distributed variable with a mean of zero and a standard deviation of 1 (see Figure 13.4.)

The stock is assumed to pay no dividends in the basic Black-Scholes-Merton model. The European option price depends on five variables: S_0, K, r, σ, and T. Of these, two (K and T) are properties of the option and two (S_0 and r) are market variables that can be readily observed. Only the volatility σ causes any problems when the formula is used. Section 13.3 explains how volatility can be estimated from historical data. Section 13.9 explains how volatility can be implied from the market prices of options.

You should make sure you understand the no-arbitrage arguments in Section 13.6. They are similar to the no-arbitrage arguments used in Chapter 12 to price options when there is one-step binomial tree. The difference is that in this case the portfolio that is set up remains riskless for only a very short (theoretically an infinitesimally short) period of time.

Another important section is Section 13.8. This extends the risk-neutral valuation ideas introduced in Chapter 12. Make sure you understand how risk-neutral valuation can be used to get the

$$f = S_0 - Ke^{-rT}$$

formula for valuing a forward contract with delivery price K. The Black-Scholes-Merton formula can be derived using risk-neutral valuation. The methodology is analogous to the methodology for valuing a forward contract with delivery price K, but the math is much more involved.

The last part of the chapter discusses how the Black-Scholes-Merton formula can be modified to allow for dividends. The basic approach is to calculate D, the present value of the dividends that will be paid during the life of the option. The variable S_0 is then replaced by $S_0 - D$ in the Black-Scholes-Merton formula. Black's approximation for valuing American call options involves setting the price equal to the greater of the prices of two European call options. The first expires at the same time as the American option; the second expires just before the final ex-dividend date (i.e., the ex-dividend date that is closest to, but before, the American option's maturity).

The Black-Scholes-Merton model makes the same assumptions as the binomial model in Chapter 12. As the appendix to Chapter 12 indicates, the price given by the binomial model for a European option converges to the Black-Scholes-Merton price as the number of steps is increased.

Software

The Equity_FX_Indx_Fut_Calc worksheet of DG400f.xls allows you to value options using the Black-Scholes-Merton model and to calculate implied volatilities. You should choose Black-Scholes – European as the *Option Type*. By checking the *Implied Volatility* box you can calculate the implied volatility from the price in cell D20. The answer appears in cell D6. To investigate the convergence of the binomial tree to the Black-Scholes price you can use the CRR convergence worksheet in DG400f Applications.xls. Enter FALSE in the IsAmerican cell (B16) so that a European option is being valued by the tree.

Answers to Practice Questions

Problem 13.8.
A stock price is currently $40. Assume that the expected return from the stock is 15% and its volatility is 25%. What is the probability distribution for the rate of return (with continuous compounding) earned over a one-year period?

In this case $\mu = 0.15$ and $\sigma = 0.25$. From equation (13.4) the probability distribution for the rate of return over a one-year period with continuous compounding is:

$$\phi\left(0.15 - \frac{0.25^2}{2}, \ 0.25^2\right)$$

i.e.,

$$\phi(0.11875, \ 0.25^2)$$

The expected value of the return is 11.875% per annum and the standard deviation is 25.0% per annum.

Problem 13.9.
A stock price has an expected return of 16% and a volatility of 35%. The current price is $38.
   a) What is the probability that a European call option on the stock with an exercise price of

$40 and a maturity date in six months will be exercised?

b) *What is the probability that a European put option on the stock with the same exercise price and maturity will be exercised?*

a) The required probability is the probability of the stock price being above $40 in six months time. Suppose that the stock price in six months is S_T. The probability distribution of $\ln S_T$ is

$$\phi\left\{\ln 38 + \left(0.16 - \frac{0.35^2}{2}\right)0.5,\ 0.35^2 \times 0.5\right\}$$

i.e.,

$$\phi(3.687,\ 0.247^2)$$

Since $\ln 40 = 3.689$, the required probability is

$$1 - N\left(\frac{3.689 - 3.687}{0.247}\right) = 1 - N(0.008)$$

From normal distribution tables $N(0.008) = 0.5032$ so that the required probability is 0.4968.

b) In this case the required probability is the probability of the stock price being less than $40 in six months. It is

$$1 - 0.4968 = 0.5032$$

Problem 13.10.

Prove that, with the notation in the chapter, a 95% confidence interval for S_T is between

$$S_0 e^{(\mu - \sigma^2/2)T - 1.96\sigma\sqrt{T}} \qquad \text{and} \qquad S_0 e^{(\mu - \sigma^2/2)T + 1.96\sigma\sqrt{T}}$$

From equation (13.2), $\ln S_T$ has the distribution

$$\phi\left\{\ln S_0 + \left(\mu - \frac{\sigma^2}{2}\right)T,\ \sigma^2 T\right\}$$

95% confidence intervals for $\ln S_T$ are therefore

$$\ln S_0 + (\mu - \frac{\sigma^2}{2})T - 1.96\sigma\sqrt{T}$$

and

$$\ln S_0 + (\mu - \frac{\sigma^2}{2})T + 1.96\sigma\sqrt{T}$$

95% confidence intervals for S_T are therefore

$$e^{\ln S_0 + (\mu - \sigma^2/2)T - 1.96\sigma\sqrt{T}} \qquad \text{and} \qquad e^{\ln S_0 + (\mu - \sigma^2/2)T + 1.96\sigma\sqrt{T}}$$

i.e.

$$S_0 e^{(\mu-\sigma^2/2)T-1.96\sigma\sqrt{T}} \qquad \text{and} \qquad S_0 e^{(\mu-\sigma^2/2)T+1.96\sigma\sqrt{T}}$$

Problem 13.11.

A portfolio manager announces that the average of the returns realized in each of the last 10 years is 20% per annum. In what respect is this statement misleading?

This problem relates to the material in Section 13.2 and Business Snapshot 13.1. The statement is misleading in that a certain sum of money, say $1,000, when invested for 10 years in the fund would have realized a return (with annual compounding) of less than 20% per annum.
The average of the returns realized in each year is always greater than the return per annum (with annual compounding) realized over 10 years. The first is an arithmetic average of the returns in each year; the second is a geometric average of these returns.

Problem 13.12.

Assume that a non-dividend-paying stock has an expected return of μ and a volatility of σ. An innovative financial institution has just announced that it will trade a derivative that pays off a dollar amount equal to

$$\frac{1}{T}\ln\left(\frac{S_T}{S_0}\right)$$

at time T. The variables S_0 and S_T denote the values of the stock price at time zero and time T.
   a) *Describe the payoff from this derivative.*
   b) *Use risk-neutral valuation to calculate the price of the derivative at time zero.*

a) The derivative will pay off a dollar amount equal to the continuously compounded return on the security between times 0 and T.

b) The expected value of $\ln(S_T / S_0)$ is, from equation (13.4), $(\mu-\sigma^2/2)T$. The expected payoff from the derivative is therefore $\mu-\sigma^2/2$. In a risk-neutral world this becomes $r-\sigma^2/2$. The value of the derivative at time zero is therefore:

$$\left(r-\frac{\sigma^2}{2}\right)e^{-rT}$$

Problem 13.13.

What is the price of a European call option on a non-dividend-paying stock when the stock price is $52, the strike price is $50, the risk-free interest rate is 12% per annum, the volatility is 30% per annum, and the time to maturity is three months?

In this case, $S_0 = 52$, $K = 50$, $r = 0.12$, $\sigma = 0.30$, and $T = 0.25$.

$$d_1 = \frac{\ln(52/50)+(0.12+0.3^2/2)0.25}{0.30\sqrt{0.25}} = 0.5365$$

$$d_2 = d_1 - 0.30\sqrt{0.25} = 0.3865$$

The price of the European call is
$$52N(0.5365) - 50e^{-0.12 \times 0.25} N(0.3865)$$

$$= 52 \times 0.7042 - 50e^{-0.03} \times 0.6504$$

$$= 5.06$$

or $5.06.

Problem 13.14.
What is the price of a European put option on a non-dividend-paying stock when the stock price is $69, the strike price is $70, the risk-free interest rate is 5% per annum, the volatility is 35% per annum, and the time to maturity is six months?

In this case, $S_0 = 69$, $K = 70$, $r = 0.05$, $\sigma = 0.35$, and $T = 0.5$.
$$d_1 = \frac{\ln(69/70) + (0.05 + 0.35^2/2) \times 0.5}{0.35\sqrt{0.5}} = 0.1666$$
$$d_2 = d_1 - 0.35\sqrt{0.5} = -0.0809$$
The price of the European put is
$$70e^{-0.05 \times 0.5} N(0.0809) - 69N(-0.1666)$$

$$= 70e^{-0.025} \times 0.5323 - 69 \times 0.4338$$

$$= 6.40$$

or $6.40.

Problem 13.15.
A call option on a non-dividend-paying stock has a market price of $2.50. The stock price is $15, the exercise price is $13, the time to maturity is three months, and the risk-free interest rate is 5% per annum. What is the implied volatility?

In the case $c = 2.5$, $S_0 = 15$, $K = 13$, $T = 0.25$, $r = 0.05$. The implied volatility must be calculated using an iterative procedure.
A volatility of 0.2 (or 20% per annum) gives $c = 2.20$. A volatility of 0.3 gives $c = 2.32$. A volatility of 0.4 gives $c = 2.507$. A volatility of 0.39 gives $c = 2.487$. By interpolation the implied volatility is about 0.396 or 39.6% per annum.
The implied volatility can also be calculated using DerivaGem. Select equity as the Underlying Type in the first worksheet of DG400f.xls. Select Black-Scholes European as the Option Type. Input stock price as 15, the risk-free rate as 5%, time to exercise as 0.25, and exercise price as 13. Leave the dividend table blank because we are assuming no dividends. Select the button corresponding to call. Select the implied volatility button. Input the Price as 2.5 in the second half of the option data table. Hit the *Enter* key and click on calculate. DerivaGem will show the volatility of the option as 39.64%.

Problem 13.16.
Show that the Black–Scholes–Merton formula for a call option gives a price that tends to $\max(S_0 - K, 0)$ *as* $T \to 0$.

$$d_1 = \frac{\ln(S_0/K) + (r + \sigma^2/2)T}{\sigma\sqrt{T}}$$

$$= \frac{\ln(S_0/K)}{\sigma\sqrt{T}} + \frac{r + \sigma^2/2}{\sigma}\sqrt{T}$$

As $T \to 0$, the second term on the right hand side tends to zero. The first term tends to $+\infty$ if $\ln(S_0/K) > 0$ and to $-\infty$ if $\ln(S_0/K) < 0$. Since $\ln(S_0/K) > 0$ when $S_0 > K$ and $\ln(S_0/K) < 0$ when $S_0 < K$, it follows that

$d_1 \to \infty$ as $T \to 0$ when $S_0 > K$
$d_1 \to -\infty$ as $T \to 0$ when $S_0 < K$

Similarly

$d_2 \to \infty$ as $T \to 0$ when $S_0 > K$
$d_2 \to -\infty$ as $T \to 0$ when $S_0 < K$

Under the Black-Scholes-Merton formula the call price, c is given by:
$$c = S_0 N(d_1) - Ke^{-rT} N(d_2)$$
From the above results, when $S_0 > K$, $N(d_1) \to 1.0$ and $N(d_2) \to 1.0$ as $T \to 0$ so that $c \to S_0 - K$. Also, when $S_0 < K$, $N(d_1) \to 0$ and $N(d_2) \to 0$ as $T \to 0$ so that $c \to 0$. These results show that $c \to \max(S_0 - K, 0)$ as $T \to 0$.

Problem 13.17.
Explain carefully why Black's approach to evaluating an American call option on a dividend-paying stock may give an approximate answer even when only one dividend is anticipated. Does the answer given by Black's approach understate or overstate the true option value? Explain your answer.

Black's approach in effect assumes that the holder of option must decide at time zero whether it is a European option maturing at time t_n (the final ex-dividend date) or a European option maturing at time T. In fact, the holder of the option has more flexibility than this. The holder can choose to exercise at time t_n if the stock price at that time is above some level but not otherwise. Furthermore, if the option is not exercised at time t_n, it can still be exercised at time T.
It appears that Black's approach should understate the true option value. This is because the holder of the option has more alternative strategies for deciding when to exercise the option than the two strategies implicitly assumed by the approach. These alternative strategies add value to

the option.
However, this is not the whole story! The standard approach to valuing either an American or a European option on a stock paying a single dividend applies the volatility to the stock price less the present value of the dividend. (The procedure for valuing an American option is explained in Chapter 18.) Black's approach when considering exercise just prior to the dividend date applies the volatility to the stock price itself. Black's approach therefore assumes more stock price variability than the standard approach in some of its calculations. In some circumstances it can give a higher price than the standard approach.

Problem 13.18.

Consider an American call option on a stock. The stock price is $70, the time to maturity is eight months, the risk-free rate of interest is 10% per annum, the exercise price is $65, and the volatility is 32%. A dividend of $1 is expected after three months and again after six months. Use the results in the appendix to show that it can never be optimal to exercise the option on either of the two dividend dates. Use DerivaGem to calculate the price of the option.

With the notation in the text
$$D_1 = D_2 = 1, \quad t_1 = 0.25, \quad t_2 = 0.50, \quad T = 0.6667, \quad r = 0.1 \quad \text{and} \quad K = 65$$

$$K(1-e^{-r(T-t_2)}) = 65(1-e^{-0.1\times0.1667}) = 1.07$$

Hence
$$D_2 < K(1-e^{-r(T-t_2)})$$

Also:
$$K(1-e^{-r(t_2-t_1)}) = 65(1-e^{-0.1\times0.25}) = 1.60$$

Hence:
$$D_1 < K(1-e^{-r(t_2-t_1)})$$

It follows from the conditions established in the Appendix to Chapter 13 that the option should never be exercised early. The option can therefore be value as a European option.
The present value of the dividends is
$$1\times e^{-0.25\times0.1} + 1\times e^{-0.50\times0.1} = 1.9265$$

Also:
$$S_0 = 68.0735, \quad K = 65, \quad \sigma = 0.32, \quad r = 0.1, \quad T = 0.6667$$

$$d_1 = \frac{\ln(68.0735/65) + (0.1+0.32^2/2)0.6667}{0.32\sqrt{0.6667}} = 0.5626$$

$$d_2 = d_1 - 0.32\sqrt{0.6667} = 0.3013$$

$$N(d_1) = 0.7131, \quad N(d_2) = 0.6184$$

and the call price is
$$68.0735\times0.7131 - 65e^{-0.1\times0.6667}\times0.6184 = 10.94$$

or $10.94.
DerivaGem can be used to calculate the price of this option. Select equity as the Underlying Type in the first worksheet of DG400f.xls. Select Black-Scholes European as the Option Type.

Input stock price as 70, the volatility as 32%, the risk-free rate as 10%, time to exercise as =8/12, and exercise price as 65. In the dividend table, enter the times of dividends as 0.25 and 0.50, and the amounts of the dividends in each case as 1. Select the button corresponding to call. Hit the *Enter* key and click on calculate. DerivaGem will show the value of the option as $10.942.

Problem 13.19.

A stock price is currently $50 and the risk-free interest rate is 5%. Use the DerivaGem software to translate the following table of European call options on the stock into a table of implied volatilities, assuming no dividends. Are the option prices consistent with the assumptions underlying Black–Scholes–Merton?

Stock Price	Maturity = 3 months	Maturity = 6 months	Maturity = 12 months
54	7.00	8.30	10.50
50	3.50	5.20	7.50
55	1.60	2.90	5.10

Using DerivaGem, we obtain the following table of implied volatilities

Stock Price	Maturity = 3 months	Maturity = 6 months	Maturity = 12 months
54	37.78	34.99	34.02
50	32.12	32.78	32.03
55	31.98	30.77	30.45

To calculate first number, select equity as the Underlying Type in the first worksheet of DG400f.xls. Select Black-Scholes European as the Option Type. Input stock price as 50, the risk-free rate as 5%, time to exercise as 0.25, and exercise price as 45. Leave the dividend table blank because we are assuming no dividends. Select the button corresponding to call. Select the implied volatility button. Input the Price as 7.0 in the second half of the option data table. Hit the *Enter* key and click on calculate. DerivaGem will show the volatility of the option as 37.78%. Change the strike price and time to exercise and recompute to calculate the rest of the numbers in the table.

The option prices are not exactly consistent with Black–Scholes–Merton. If they were, the implied volatilities would be all the same. We usually find in practice that low strike price options on a stock have higher implied volatilities than high strike price options on the same stock. This phenomenon is discussed in Chapter 19.

Problem 13.20.

Show that the Black–Scholes–Merton formulas for call and put options satisfy put–call parity.

The Black–Scholes–Merton formula for a European call option is

$$c = S_0 N(d_1) - Ke^{-rT} N(d_2)$$

so that

$$c + Ke^{-rT} = S_0 N(d_1) - Ke^{-rT} N(d_2) + Ke^{-rT}$$

or

$$c + Ke^{-rT} = S_0 N(d_1) + Ke^{-rT}[1 - N(d_2)]$$

or

$$c + Ke^{-rT} = S_0 N(d_1) + Ke^{-rT} N(-d_2)$$

The Black–Scholes–Merton formula for a European put option is

$$p = Ke^{-rT} N(-d_2) - S_0 N(-d_1)$$

so that

$$p + S_0 = Ke^{-rT} N(-d_2) - S_0 N(-d_1) + S_0$$

or

$$p + S_0 = Ke^{-rT} N(-d_2) + S_0[1 - N(-d_1)]$$

or

$$p + S_0 = Ke^{-rT} N(-d_2) + S_0 N(d_1)$$

This shows that the put–call parity result

$$c + Ke^{-rT} = p + S_0$$

holds.

Problem 13.21.

Show that the probability that a European call option will be exercised in a risk-neutral world is, with the notation introduced in this chapter, $N(d_2)$. What is an expression for the value of a derivative that pays off \$100 if the price of a stock at time T is greater than K?

The probability that the call option will be exercised is the probability that $S_T > K$ where S_T is the stock price at time T. In a risk neutral world the probability distribution of $\ln S_T$ is

$$\phi\{\ln S_0 + (r - \sigma^2/2)T, \sigma^2 T\}$$

The probability that $S_T > K$ is the same as the probability that $\ln S_T > \ln K$. This is

$$1 - N\left[\frac{\ln K - \ln S_0 - (r - \sigma^2/2)T}{\sigma\sqrt{T}}\right]$$

$$= N\left[\frac{\ln(S_0/K) + (r - \sigma^2/2)T}{\sigma\sqrt{T}}\right]$$

$$= N(d_2)$$

The expected value at time T in a risk neutral world of a derivative security which pays off \$100 when $S_T > K$ is therefore

$$100N(d_2)$$

From risk neutral valuation the value of the security is

$$100e^{-rT} N(d_2)$$

CHAPTER 14
Employee Stock Options

First you should make sure you understand how employee stock options work and why they are different from regular stock options. The main features of a typical stock option arrangement are listed at the beginning of Section 14.1. Employee stock options tend to be exercised earlier than they would be if they were regular stock options because employees are not allowed to sell their options.

Whether employee stock options align the interests of executives and shareholders is somewhat controversial. If the share price of the company goes up, the shareholders do well and so do the executives. However, if the share price goes down the shareholders lose money, but the executives merely fail to make a gain. It can be argued that granting shares rather than options to executives better aligns their interests to the interests of shareholders. A general problem with stock option (or stock) compensation is that executives have more information about the company than the rest of the market and can time their trades (or option exercises) accordingly.

It used to be the case that the cost to the company of granting at-the-money options was not recognized in the company's financial statements. We then went through a period when the cost had to be reported in the footnotes. We are now in the position where the cost must be expensed on the income statement. This has made employee stock option compensation somewhat less popular than it used to be. The type of compensation given to executives is now less driven by the accounting treatment and some companies use nontraditional plans. For example, the strike price sometimes moves up and down with a reference index (such as the S&P 500) so that the company has to outperform the reference index for the options to move in the money.

The most popular approach to valuing employee stock options is to use Black-Scholes-Merton model with the life of the options set equal to the expected time for which the option will remain active. This is the expected time until the option expires. It might expire because a) it is exercised, b) it reaches the end of its life, or c) it is canceled when the employee leaves the company. The approach does not have theoretical validity, but seems to work reasonably well. If the early exercise behavior of employees can be modeled, more sophisticated approaches involving binomial trees can be used.

Some companies have in the past engaged in an illegal practice known as backdating. Suppose that the stock price is now $40, but it was $30 three weeks ago. It is tempting to pretend that the decision to issue at-the-money options was made three weeks ago. This increases the value of the options to the recipients without increasing the expense recorded in the company's financial statements. Academic research uncovered the widespread use of this practice. The practice became less common when the SEC required companies to report option grants within two business days.

Software
A simple way of valuing employee stock options assumes that exercise of vested stock options

takes place when the ratio of the stock price to the strike price reaches some multiple. Software for implementing this is on the author's website: www-2.rotman.utoronto.ca/~hull/ESOPS

Answers to Practice Questions

Problem 14.8.
Explain how you would do the analysis similar to that of Yermack and Lie to determine whether the backdating of stock options was happening..

It would be necessary to look at returns on each stock in the sample around the reported employee stock option grant date. One could designate Day 0 as the grant date and look at returns on each stock each day from Day –30 to Day +30. The returns relative to Day 0 would then be averaged across the stocks.

Problem 14.9.
On May 31 a company's stock price is $70. One million shares are outstanding. An executive exercises 100,000 stock options with a strike price of $50. What is the impact of this on the stock price?

There should be no impact on the stock price because the stock price will already reflect the dilution expected from the executive's exercise decision.

Problem 14.10.
The notes accompanying a company's financial statements say: "Our executive stock options last 10 years and vest after four years. We valued the options granted this year using the Black–Scholes–Merton model with an expected life of 5 years and a volatility of 20%. "What does this mean? Discuss the modeling approach used by the company.

The notes indicate that the Black-Scholes-Merton model was used to produce the valuation with the option life being set equal to 5 years and the stock price volatility being set equal to 20%.

Problem 14.11.
A company has granted 500,000 options to its executives. The stock price and strike price are both $40. The options last for 12 years and vest after four years. The company decides to value the options using an expected life of five years and a volatility of 30% per annum. The company pays no dividends and the risk-free rate is 4%. What will the company report as an expense for the options on its income statement?

The options are valued using the Black-Scholes-Merton model with $S_0 = 40$, $K = 40$, $T = 5$, $\sigma = 0.3$ and $r = 0.04$. The value of each option is $13.585. The total expense reported is $500,000 \times \$13.585$ or $6.792 million.

Problem 14.12.
A company's CFO says: "The accounting treatment of stock options is crazy. We granted

10,000,000 at-the-money stock options to our employees last year when the stock price was $30. We estimated the value of each option on the grant date to be $5. At our year end the stock price had fallen to $4, but we were still stuck with a $50 million charge to the P&L." Discuss.

The problem is that under the current rules the options are valued only once—on the grant date. Arguably it would make sense to treat the options in the same way as other derivatives entered into by the company and revalue them on each reporting date. However, this does not happen under the current accounting rules unless the options are settled in cash.

CHAPTER 15
Options on Stock Indices and Currencies

If you have a good understanding of Chapter 13, this chapter should present few problems. The chapter provides some examples of how index options and foreign currency options are used and then moves on to extend the results from Chapter 13 so that they can be used to value these options when they are European.

As explained in Section 15.1, index put options can be used to provide portfolio insurance (i.e., ensure that the value of a portfolio does not fall below a certain level). The value of the assets underlying the option should equal the beta of the portfolio times the value of the assets being insured. The strike price should be chosen so that when the index equals the strike price the value of portfolio can be expected to be equal to the insured value. (This is a capital asset pricing model calculation.)

Section 15.2 introduces range forward contracts. These are products designed to ensure that the exchange rate applicable to a foreign currency transaction in the future lies between two levels. Range forward contracts can be created by buying a put and selling a call (Figure 15.1a) or buying a call and selling a put (Figure 15.1b)

The key material for valuation is in Section 15.3. This shows that, if an investment asset provides a yield at rate q then the Black-Scholes-Merton formula applies for a European option with S_0 replaced by $S_0 e^{-qT}$ (see equations 15.4 and 15.5). What is more, the lower bounds on option prices in Chapter 10 apply with S_0 replaced by $S_0 e^{-qT}$ (see equations 15.1 and 15.2). Also, put-call parity applies with S_0 replaced by $S_0 e^{-qT}$ (see equation 15.3).

For American options, we can use a binomial tree, but must design the tree so that on average the asset price grows at $r - q$ rather than r in the risk-neutral world represented by the tree. (A return of q is provided by the dividends and so the index needs to grow at $r-q$ for the total return to be r.) This means that the growth factor variable a is defined as $e^{(r-q)\Delta t}$ rather than as $e^{r\Delta t}$.

When valuing options on stock indices we set q equal to the average dividend yield on the index during the life of the option. Most exchange-traded options on stock indices are European. An exception is the OEX (which is an American option on the S&P 100).

When valuing options on currencies we set q equal to the foreign risk-free rate, r_f. Make sure you understand why a currency is analogous to an asset providing a known yield. The key point is that interest income on the foreign currency is earned in the foreign currency not the domestic currency and the value of the income is therefore proportional to the value of the foreign currency. As equations (15.10) and (15.11) show, the pricing formulas for European currency options can be expressed in terms of forward exchange rates rather than spot exchange rates. It is then not necessary to know what the foreign risk-free rate, r_f, is. (All the relevant information about r_f is included in F_0.)

Software

The Equity_FX_Indx_Fut_Calc worksheet of DG400f.xls allows you to value European or American options on foreign exchange or indices.

Answers to Practice Questions

Problem 15.8.

Show that the formula in equation (15.9) for a put option to sell one unit of currency A for currency B at strike price K gives the same value as equation (15.8) for a call option to buy K units of currency B for currency A at a strike price of $1/K$.

A put option to sell one unit of currency A for K units of currency B is worth
$$Ke^{-r_B T}N(-d_2) - S_0 e^{-r_A T}N(-d_1)$$
where

$$d_1 = \frac{\ln(S_0/K) + (r_B - r_A + \sigma^2/2)T}{\sigma\sqrt{T}}$$

$$d_2 = \frac{\ln(S_0/K) + (r_B - r_A - \sigma^2/2)T}{\sigma\sqrt{T}}$$

and r_A and r_B are the risk-free rates in currencies A and B, respectively. The value of the option is measured in units of currency B. Defining $S_0^* = 1/S_0$ and $K^* = 1/K$

$$d_1 = \frac{-\ln(S_0^*/K^*) - (r_A - r_B - \sigma^2/2)T}{\sigma\sqrt{T}}$$

$$d_2 = \frac{-\ln(S_0^*/K^*) - (r_A - r_B + \sigma^2/2)T}{\sigma\sqrt{T}}$$

The put price is therefore
$$S_0 K[S_0^* e^{-r_B T}N(d_1^*) - K^* e^{-r_A T}N(d_2^*)$$
where

$$d_1^* = -d_2 = \frac{\ln(S_0^*/K^*) + (r_A - r_B + \sigma^2/2)T}{\sigma\sqrt{T}}$$

$$d_2^* = -d_1 = \frac{\ln(S_0^*/K^*) + (r_A - r_B - \sigma^2/2)T}{\sigma\sqrt{T}}$$

This shows that put option is equivalent to KS_0 call options to buy 1 unit of currency A for $1/K$ units of currency B. In this case the value of the option is measured in units of currency A. To obtain the call option value in units of currency B (the same units as the value of the put option was measured in) we must divide by S_0. This proves the result.

Problem 15.9.

A foreign currency is currently worth $1.50. The domestic and foreign risk-free interest rates are 5% and 9%, respectively. Calculate a lower bound for the value of a six-month call option on the currency with a strike price of $1.40 if it is (a) European and (b) American.

Lower bound for European option is
$$S_0 e^{-r_f T} - K e^{-rT} = 1.5 e^{-0.09 \times 0.5} - 1.4 e^{-0.05 \times 0.5} = 0.069$$
Lower bound for American option is
$$S_0 - K = 0.10$$

Problem 15.10.

Consider a stock index currently standing at 250. The dividend yield on the index is 4% per annum, and the risk-free rate is 6% per annum. A three-month European call option on the index with a strike price of 245 is currently worth $10. What is the value of a three-month put option on the index with a strike price of 245?

In this case $S_0 = 250$, $q = 0.04$, $r = 0.06$, $T = 0.25$, $K = 245$, and $c = 10$. Using put–call parity
$$c + K e^{-rT} = p + S_0 e^{-qT}$$
or
$$p = c + K e^{-rT} - S_0 e^{-qT}$$

Substituting:
$$p = 10 + 245 e^{-0.25 \times 0.06} - 250 e^{-0.25 \times 0.04} = 3.84$$
The put price is 3.84.

Problem 15.11.

An index currently stands at 696 and has a volatility of 30% per annum. The risk-free rate of interest is 7% per annum and the index provides a dividend yield of 4% per annum. Calculate the value of a three-month European put with an exercise price of 700.

In this case $S_0 = 696$, $K = 700$, $r = 0.07$, $\sigma = 0.3$, $T = 0.25$ and $q = 0.04$. The option can be valued using equation (15.5).
$$d_1 = \frac{\ln(696/700) + (0.07 - 0.04 + 0.09/2) \times 0.25}{0.3\sqrt{0.25}} = 0.0868$$
$$d_2 = d_1 - 0.3\sqrt{0.25} = -0.0632$$

and
$$N(-d_1) = 0.4654, \quad N(-d_2) = 0.5252$$
The value of the put, p, is given by:
$$p = 700 e^{-0.07 \times 0.25} \times 0.5252 - 696 e^{-0.04 \times 0.25} \times 0.4654 = 40.6$$
i.e., it is $40.6.

Problem 15.12.

Show that if C is the price of an American call with exercise price K and maturity T on a stock paying a dividend yield of q, and P is the price of an American put on the same stock with the same strike price and exercise date,

$$S_0 e^{-qT} - K < C - P < S_0 - Ke^{-rT}$$

where S_0 is the stock price, r is the risk-free rate, and $r > 0$. (Hint: To obtain the first half of the inequality, consider possible values of:

Portfolio A; a European call option plus an amount K invested at the risk-free rate

Portfolio B: an American put option plus e^{-qT} of stock with dividends being reinvested in the stock

To obtain the second half of the inequality, consider possible values of:

Portfolio C: an American call option plus an amount Ke^{-rT} invested at the risk-free rate

Portfolio D: a European put option plus one stock with dividends being reinvested in the stock)

Following the hint, we first consider

Portfolio A: A European call option plus an amount K invested at the risk-free rate

Portfolio B: An American put option plus e^{-qT} of stock with dividends being reinvested in the stock.

Portfolio A is worth $c + K$ while portfolio B is worth $P + S_0 e^{-qT}$. If the put option is exercised at time $\tau (0 \le \tau < T)$, portfolio B becomes:

$$K - S_\tau + S_\tau e^{-q(T-\tau)} \le K$$

where S_τ is the stock price at time τ. Portfolio A is worth

$$c + Ke^{r\tau} \ge K$$

Hence, portfolio A is worth at least as much as portfolio B. If both portfolios are held to maturity (time T), portfolio A is worth

$$\max(S_T - K, 0) + Ke^{rT}$$
$$= \max(S_T, K) + K(e^{rT} - 1)$$

Portfolio B is worth $\max(S_T, K)$. Hence portfolio A is worth more than portfolio B. Because portfolio A is worth at least as much as portfolio B in all circumstances

$$P + S_0 e^{-qT} \le c + K$$

Because $c \le C$:

$$P + S_0 e^{-qT} \le C + K$$

or

$$S_0 e^{-qT} - K \le C - P$$

This proves the first part of the inequality.

For the second part consider:

Portfolio C: An American call option plus an amount Ke^{-rT} invested at the risk-free rate

Portfolio D: A European put option plus one stock with dividends being reinvested in the stock.

Portfolio C is worth $C + Ke^{-rT}$ while portfolio D is worth $p + S_0$. If the call option is exercised at time $\tau(0 \le \tau < T)$ portfolio C becomes:

$$S_\tau - K + Ke^{-r(T-\tau)} < S_\tau$$

while portfolio D is worth

$$p + S_\tau e^{q(\tau-t)} \ge S_\tau$$

Hence portfolio D is worth more than portfolio C. If both portfolios are held to maturity (time T), portfolio C is worth $\max(S_T, K)$ while portfolio D is worth

$$\max(K - S_T, 0) + S_T e^{qT} = \max(S_T, K) + S_T(e^{qT} - 1)$$

Hence portfolio D is worth at least as much as portfolio C.
Since portfolio D is worth at least as much as portfolio C in all circumstances:

$$C + Ke^{-rT} \le p + S_0$$

Since $p \le P$:

$$C + Ke^{-rT} \le P + S_0$$

or

$$C - P \le S_0 - Ke^{-rT}$$

This proves the second part of the inequality. Hence:

$$S_0 e^{-qT} - K \le C - P \le S_0 - Ke^{-rT}$$

Problem 15.13.
Show that a European call option on a currency has the same price as the corresponding European put option on the currency when the forward price equals the strike price.

This follows from put–call parity and the relationship between the forward price, F_0, and the spot price, S_0

$$c + Ke^{-rT} = p + S_0 e^{-r_f T}$$

and

$$F_0 = S_0 e^{(r-r_f)T}$$

so that

$$c + Ke^{-rT} = p + F_0 e^{-rT}$$

If $K = F_0$ this reduces to $c = p$. The result that $c = p$ when $K = F_0$ is true for options on all underlying assets, not just options on currencies. An at-the-money option is sometimes defined as one where $K = F_0$ (or $c = p$) rather than one where $K = S_0$.

Problem 15.14.
Would you expect the volatility of a stock index to be greater or less than the volatility of a typical stock? Explain your answer.

The volatility of a stock index can be expected to be less than the volatility of a typical stock. This is because some risk (i.e., return uncertainty) is diversified away when a portfolio of stocks is created. In capital asset pricing model terminology, there exists systematic and unsystematic risk in the returns from an individual stock. However, in a stock index, unsystematic risk has been diversified away and only the systematic risk contributes to volatility.

Problem 15.15.

Does the cost of portfolio insurance increase or decrease as the beta of a portfolio increases? Explain your answer.

The cost of portfolio insurance increases as the beta of the portfolio increases. This is because portfolio insurance involves the purchase of a put option on the portfolio. As beta increases, the volatility of the portfolio increases causing the cost of the put option to increase. When index options are used to provide portfolio insurance, both the number of options required and the strike price increase as beta increases.

Problem 15.16.

Suppose that a portfolio is worth $60 million and the S&P 500 is at 1200. If the value of the portfolio mirrors the value of the index, what options should be purchased to provide protection against the value of the portfolio falling below $54 million in one year's time?

If the value of the portfolio mirrors the value of the index, the index can be expected to have dropped by 10% when the value of the portfolio drops by 10%. Hence when the value of the portfolio drops to $54 million the value of the index can be expected to be 1080. This indicates that put options with an exercise price of 1,080 should be purchased. The options should be on:

$$\frac{60,000,000}{1200} = \$50,000$$

times the index. Each option contract is for $100 times the index. Hence 500 contracts should be purchased.

Problem 15.17.

Consider again the situation in Problem 15.16. Suppose that the portfolio has a beta of 2.0, the risk-free interest rate is 5% per annum, and the dividend yield on both the portfolio and the index is 3% per annum. What options should be purchased to provide protection against the value of the portfolio falling below $54 million in one year's time?

When the value of the portfolio falls to $54 million the holder of the portfolio makes a capital loss of 10%. After dividends are taken into account the loss is 7% during the year. This is 12% below the risk-free interest rate. According to the capital asset pricing model, the expected excess return of the portfolio above the risk-free rate equals beta times the expected excess return of the market above the risk-free rate.

Therefore, when the portfolio provides a return 12% below the risk-free interest rate, the market's expected return is 6% below the risk-free interest rate. As the index can be assumed to have a beta of 1.0, this is also the excess expected return (including dividends) from the index. The expected return from the index is therefore -1% per annum. Since the index provides a 3% per annum dividend yield, the expected movement in the index is -4%. Thus when the portfolio's value is $54 million the expected value of the index is $0.96 \times 1,200 = 1,152$. Hence European put options should be purchased with an exercise price of 1,152. Their maturity date should be in one year.

The number of options required is twice the number required in Problem 15.16. This is because we wish to protect a portfolio which is twice as sensitive to changes in market conditions as the portfolio in Problem 15.16. Hence options on $100,000 (or 1,000 contracts) should be purchased. To check that the answer is correct consider what happens when the value of the portfolio declines by 20% to $48 million. The return including dividends is -17%. This is 22% less than the risk-free interest rate. The index can be expected to provide a return (including dividends) which is 11% less than the risk-free interest rate, i.e. a return of -6%. The index can therefore be expected to drop by 9% to 1,092. The payoff from the put options is $(1,152\text{-}1,092)\times100,000 = \$6$ million. This is exactly what is required to restore the value of the portfolio to $54 million.

Problem 15.18.
An index currently stands at 1,500. European call and put options with a strike price of 1,400 and time to maturity of six months have market prices of 154.00 and 34.25, respectively. The six-month risk-free rate is 5%. What is the implied dividend yield?

The implied dividend yield is the value of q that satisfies the put–call parity equation. It is the value of q that solves
$$154+1400e^{-0.05\times0.5} = 34.25+1500e^{-0.5q}$$
This is 1.99%.

Problem 15.19.
A total return index tracks the return, including dividends, on a certain portfolio. Explain how you would value (a) forward contracts and (b) European options on the index.

A total return index behaves like a stock paying no dividends. In a risk-neutral world it can be expected to grow on average at the risk-free rate. Forward contracts and options on total return indices should be valued in the same way as forward contracts and options on non-dividend-paying stocks.

Problem 15.20.
What is the put–call parity relationship for European currency options

The put–call parity relationship for European currency options is
$$c + Ke^{-rT} = p + Se^{-r_fT}$$
To prove this result, the two portfolios to consider are:
Portfolio A: one call option plus one zero-coupon domestic bond which will be worth K at time T.
Portfolio B: one put option plus one foreign currency bond that will be worth one unit of the foreign currency at time T.
Both portfolios are worth $\max(S_T, K)$ at time T. They must therefore be worth the same today. The result follows.

Problem 15.21.
Can an option on the yen-euro exchange rate be created from two options, one on the dollar-euro exchange rate, and the other on the dollar-yen exchange rate? Explain your answer.

There is no way of doing this. A natural idea is to create an option to exchange K euros for one yen from an option to exchange Y dollars for 1 yen and an option to exchange K euros for Y dollars. The problem with this is that it assumes that either both options are exercised or that neither option is exercised. There are always some circumstances where the first option is in-the-money at expiration while the second is not and vice versa.

Problem 15.22.
Prove the results in equation (15.1), (15.2), and (15.3) using the portfolios indicated.

In portfolio A, the cash, if it is invested at the risk-free interest rate, will grow to K at time T. If $S_T > K$, the call option is exercised at time T and portfolio A is worth S_T. If $S_T < K$, the call option expires worthless and the portfolio is worth K. Hence, at time T, portfolio A is worth

$$\max(S_T, K)$$

Because of the reinvestment of dividends, portfolio B becomes one share at time T. It is, therefore, worth S_T at this time. It follows that portfolio A is always worth as much as, and is sometimes worth more than, portfolio B at time T. In the absence of arbitrage opportunities, this must also be true today. Hence,

$$c + Ke^{-rT} \geq S_0 e^{-qT}$$

or

$$c \geq S_0 e^{-qT} - Ke^{-rT}$$

This proves equation (15.1)

In portfolio C, the reinvestment of dividends means that the portfolio is one put option plus one share at time T. If $S_T < K$, the put option is exercised at time T and portfolio C is worth K. If $S_T > K$, the put option expires worthless and the portfolio is worth S_T. Hence, at time T, portfolio C is worth

$$\max(S_T, K)$$

Portfolio D is worth K at time T. It follows that portfolio C is always worth as much as, and is sometimes worth more than, portfolio D at time T. In the absence of arbitrage opportunities, this must also be true today. Hence,

$$p + S_0 e^{-qT} \geq Ke^{-rT}$$

or

$$p \geq Ke^{-rT} - S_0 e^{-qT}$$

This proves equation (15.2)

Portfolios A and C are both worth $\max(S_T, K)$ at time T. They must, therefore, be worth the same today, and the put–call parity result in equation (15.3) follows.

CHAPTER 16
Futures Options and Black's Model

The first part of this chapter describes how futures options work. A call futures option is the right to enter into a long futures contract by a certain future date. The cash payoff when the option is exercised is $F - K$ where F is the most recent settlement futures price and K is the strike price. The exerciser also obtains a long futures contract. A put futures option is the right to enter into a short futures contract by a future date. The cash payoff when the option is exercised is $K - F$. The exerciser also obtains a short futures contract (see Examples 16.1 and 16.2). When the value of the futures contract is taken into account the payoff on a call is the excess of the futures price at the time of exercise over the strike price and the payoff on a put is the excess of the strike price over the futures price at the time of exercise.

It turns out that a futures price can be treated like an asset that provides a yield equal to the risk-free rate, r. The reason is that, because it costs nothing to enter into a futures contract, the contract must on average provide a zero return in a risk-neutral world. Hence, its expected growth rate in a risk-neutral world must be zero. This is the same as the expected growth rate for an asset providing a yield at rate r.

Bounds for futures options (equations 16.3 and 16.4), put-call parity for futures options (equation 16.1), pricing formulas for European futures options (equations 16.5 and 16.6), and binomial trees for valuing American futures options (equations 16.7 and 16.8) are all exactly the same as in Chapter 15 except that we set $q = r$. In particular, when a binomial tree is constructed for futures options, $a = e^{-(r-r)\Delta t} = 1$.

The equations to value European options on futures are known as Black's model. A European option on a futures price has the same price as a regular European option on the spot price of an asset when the futures contract and the option expire at the same time. Similarly, a European option on a forward price has the same price as a regular European option on the spot price of an asset when the forward contract and the option expire at the same time. As a result Black's model can be (and frequently is) used to value a European option on the spot price of an asset in terms the futures or forward price of the underlying asset (see Example 16.5).

As explained at the end of the chapter, exchange-traded futures options are sometimes futures-style options. These are futures contracts on the payoff from a call or a put option.

Software
The Equity_FX_Indx_Fut_Calc worksheet of DG400f.xls allows you to value European or American options on futures contracts.

Answers to Practice Questions

Problem 16.8.
Suppose you buy a put option contract on October gold futures with a strike price of $1,200 per ounce. Each contract is for the delivery of 100 ounces. What happens if you exercise when the

October futures price is $1,160?

You gain $(1,200 - 1,160) \times 100 = \$4,000$. This gain is made up of a) a short futures contract in October gold and b) a cash payoff you receive which is 100 times the excess of $1,200 over the previous settlement price. The short futures position is marked to market in the usual way until you choose to close it out.

Problem 16.9.

Suppose you sell a call option contract on April live cattle futures with a strike price of 140 cents per pound. Each contract is for the delivery of 40,000 pounds. What happens if the contract is exercised when the futures price is 145 cents?

In this case, you lose $(1.45 - 1.40) \times 40,000 = \$2,000$. The loss is made up of a) a cash payoff you have to make equal to 40,000 times the excess of the previous settlement price over the previous settlement price and b) a short April futures contract.

Problem 16.10.

Consider a two-month futures call option with a strike price of 40 when the risk-free interest rate is 10% per annum. The current futures price is 47. What is a lower bound for the value of the futures option if it is (a) European and (b) American?

Lower bound if option is European is
$$(F_0 - K)e^{-rT} = (47 - 40)e^{-0.1 \times 2/12} = 6.88$$
Lower bound if option is American is
$$F_0 - K = 7$$

Problem 16.11.

Consider a four-month futures put option with a strike price of 50 when the risk-free interest rate is 10% per annum. The current futures price is 47. What is a lower bound for the value of the futures option if it is (a) European and (b) American?

Lower bound if option is European is
$$(K - F_0)e^{-rT} = (50 - 47)e^{-0.1 \times 4/12} = 2.90$$
Lower bound if option is American is
$$K - F_0 = 3$$

Problem 16.12.

A futures price is currently 60 and its volatility is 30%. The risk-free interest rate is 8% per annum. Use a two-step binomial tree to calculate the value of a six-month European call option on the futures with a strike price of 60? If the call were American, would it ever be worth exercising it early?

In this case $u = e^{0.3 \times \sqrt{1/4}} = 1.1618$; $d = 1/u = 0.8607$; and

$$p = \frac{1 - 0.8607}{1.1618 - 0.8607} = 0.4626$$

In the tree shown in Figure S16.1 the middle number at each node is the price of the European option and the lower number is the price of the American option. The tree shows that the value of the European option is 4.3155 and the value of the American option is 4.4026. The American option should sometimes be exercised early.

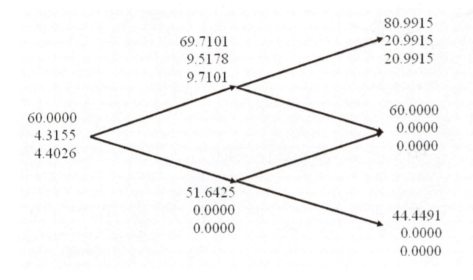

69.7101
9.5178
9.7101

80.9915
20.9915
20.9915

60.0000
4.3155
4.4026

60.0000
0.0000
0.0000

51.6425
0.0000
0.0000

44.4491
0.0000
0.0000

Figure S16.1 Tree to evaluate European and American call options in Problem 16.12

Problem 16.13.
In Problem 16.12 what value does the binomial tree give for a six-month European put option on futures with a strike price of 60? If the put were American, would it ever be worth exercising it early? Verify that the call prices calculated in Problem 16.12 and the put prices calculated here satisfy put–call parity relationships.

The parameters u, d, and p are the same as in Problem 16.12. The tree in Figure S16.2 shows that the prices of the European and American put options are the same as those calculated for call options in Problem 16.12. This illustrates a symmetry that exists for at-the-money futures options. The American option should sometimes be exercised early. Because $K = F_0$ and $c = p$, the European put–call parity result holds.

$$c + Ke^{-rT} = p + F_0 e^{-rT}$$

Also because $C = P$, $F_0 e^{-rT} < K$, and $Ke^{-rT} < F_0$ the result in equation (16.2) holds. (The first expression in equation (16.2) is negative; the middle expression is zero, and the last expression is positive.)

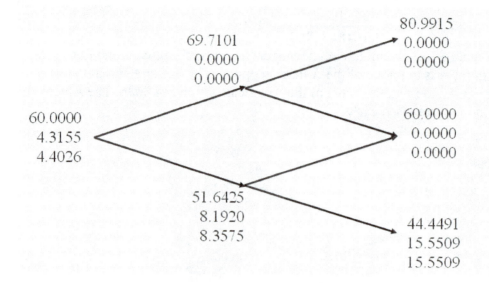

Figure S16.2 Tree to evaluate European and American put options in Problem 16.13

Problem 16.14.
A futures price is currently 25, its volatility is 30% per annum, and the risk-free interest rate is 10% per annum. What is the value of a nine-month European call on the futures with a strike price of 26?

In this case, $F_0 = 25$, $K = 26$, $\sigma = 0.3$, $r = 0.1$, $T = 0.75$

$$d_1 = \frac{\ln(F_0/K) + \sigma^2 T/2}{\sigma\sqrt{T}} = -0.0211$$

$$d_2 = \frac{\ln(F_0/K) - \sigma^2 T/2}{\sigma\sqrt{T}} = -0.2809$$

$$c = e^{-0.075}[25N(-0.0211) - 26N(-0.2809)]$$

$$= e^{-0.075}[25 \times 0.4916 - 26 \times 0.3894] = 2.01$$

Problem 16.15.
A futures price is currently 70, its volatility is 20% per annum, and the risk-free interest rate is 6% per annum. What is the value of a five-month European put on the futures with a strike price of 65?

In this case $F_0 = 70$, $K = 65$, $\sigma = 0.2$, $r = 0.06$, $T = 0.4167$

$$d_1 = \frac{\ln(F_0/K) + \sigma^2 T/2}{\sigma\sqrt{T}} = 0.6386$$

$$d_2 = \frac{\ln(F_0 / K) - \sigma^2 T / 2}{\sigma \sqrt{T}} = 0.5095$$

$$p = e^{-0.025}[65N(-0.5095) - 70N(-0.6386)]$$

$$= e^{-0.025}[65 \times 0.3052 - 70 \times 0.2615] = 1.495$$

Problem 16.16.
Suppose that a one-year futures price is currently 35. A one-year European call option and a one-year European put option on the futures with a strike price of 34 are both priced at 2 in the market. The risk-free interest rate is 10% per annum. Identify an arbitrage opportunity.

In this case

$$c + Ke^{-rT} = 2 + 34e^{-0.1 \times 1} = 32.76$$

$$p + F_0 e^{-rT} = 2 + 35e^{-0.1 \times 1} = 33.67$$

Put-call parity shows that we should buy one call, short one put and short a futures contract. This costs nothing up front. In one year, either we exercise the call or the put is exercised against us. In either case, we buy the asset for 34 and close out the futures position. The gain on the short futures position is $35 - 34 = 1$.

Problem 16.17.
"The price of an at-the-money European futures call option always equals the price of a similar at-the-money European futures put option." Explain why this statement is true.

The put price is
$$e^{-rT}[KN(-d_2) - F_0 N(-d_1)]$$
Because $N(-x) = 1 - N(x)$ for all x the put price can also be written
$$e^{-rT}[K - KN(d_2) - F_0 + F_0 N(d_1)]$$
Because $F_0 = K$ this is the same as the call price:
$$e^{-rT}[F_0 N(d_1) - KN(d_2)]$$
This result can also be proved from put–call parity showing that it is not model dependent. (See also Problems 16.12 and 16.13.)

Problem 16.18.
Suppose that a futures price is currently 30. The risk-free interest rate is 5% per annum. A three-month American futures call option with a strike price of 28 is worth 4. Calculate bounds for the price of a three-month American futures put option with a strike price of 28.

From equation (16.2), $C - P$ must lie between
$$30e^{-0.05 \times 3/12} - 28 = 1.63$$
and
$$30 - 28e^{-0.05 \times 3/12} = 2.35$$

105

Because $C = 4$ we must have $1.63 < 4 - P < 2.35$ or
$$1.65 < P < 2.37$$

Problem 16.19.
Show that if C is the price of an American call option on a futures contract when the strike price is K and the maturity is T, and P is the price of an American put on the same futures contract with the same strike price and exercise date,
$$F_0 e^{-rT} - K < C - P < F_0 - K e^{-rT}$$
where F_0 is the futures price and r is the risk-free rate. Assume that $r > 0$ and that there is no difference between forward and futures contracts. (Hint: Use an analogous approach to that indicated for Problem 15.12.)

In this case we consider
Portfolio A: A European call option on futures plus an amount K invested at the risk-free interest rate
Portfolio B: An American put option on futures plus an amount $F_0 e^{-rT}$ invested at the risk-free interest rate plus a long futures contract maturing at time T.
Following the arguments in Chapter 5 we will treat all futures contracts as forward contracts.

Portfolio A is worth $c + K$ while portfolio B is worth $P + F_0 e^{-rT}$. If the put option is exercised at time $\tau(0 \leq \tau < T)$, portfolio B is worth
$$K - F_\tau + F_0 e^{-r(T-\tau)} + F_\tau - F_0 = K + F_0 e^{-r(T-\tau)} - F_0 < K$$
at time τ where F_τ is the futures price at time τ. Portfolio A is worth
$$c + K e^{r\tau} \geq K$$
Hence Portfolio A is worth more than Portfolio B. If both portfolios are held to maturity (time T), Portfolio A is worth
$$\max(F_T - K, 0) + K e^{rT} = \max(F_T, K) + K(e^{rT} - 1)$$
Portfolio B is worth
$$\max(K - F_T, 0) + F_0 + F_T - F_0 = \max(F_T, K)$$
Hence portfolio A is worth more than portfolio B.
Because portfolio A is worth more than portfolio B in all circumstances:
$$P + F_0 e^{-r(T-t)} < c + K$$
Because $c \leq C$ it follows that
$$P + F_0 e^{-rT} < C + K$$
or
$$F_0 e^{-rT} - K < C - P$$
This proves the first part of the inequality.

For the second part of the inequality consider:
Portfolio C: An American call futures option plus an amount $K e^{-rT}$ invested at the risk-free interest rate

106

Portfolio D: A European put futures option plus an amount F_0 invested at the risk-free interest rate plus a long futures contract.

Portfolio C is worth $C + Ke^{-rT}$ while portfolio D is worth $p + F_0$. If the call option is exercised at time $\tau (0 \le \tau < T)$, portfolio C becomes:

$$F_\tau - K + Ke^{-r(T-\tau)} < F_\tau$$

while portfolio D is worth

$$p + F_0 e^{r\tau} + F_\tau - F_0 = p + F_0(e^{r\tau} - 1) + F_\tau > F_\tau$$

Hence portfolio D is worth more than portfolio C. If both portfolios are held to maturity (time T), portfolio C is worth $\max(F_T, K)$ while portfolio D is worth

$$\max(K - F_T, 0) + F_0 e^{rT} + F_T - F_0 = \max(K, F_T) + F_0(e^{rT} - 1) > \max(K, F_T)$$

Hence portfolio D is worth more than portfolio C.
Because portfolio D is worth more than portfolio C in all circumstances

$$C + Ke^{-rT} < p + F_0$$

Because $p \le P$ it follows that

$$C + Ke^{-rT} < P + F_0$$

or

$$C - P < F_0 - Ke^{-rT}$$

This proves the second part of the inequality. The result:

$$F_0 e^{-rT} - K < C - P < F_0 - Ke^{-rT}$$

has therefore been proved.

Problem 16.20.
Calculate the price of a three-month European call option on the spot price of silver. The three-month futures price is $12, the strike price is $13, the risk-free rate is 4%, and the volatility of the price of silver is 25%.

This has the same value as a three-month European call option on silver futures where the futures contract expires in three months. It can therefore be valued using equation (16.5) with $F_0 = 12$, $K = 13$, $r = 0.04$, $\sigma = 0.25$ and $T = 0.25$. The value is 0.244.

CHAPTER 17
The Greek Letters

This chapter considers a trader who is responsible for trading financial instruments dependent on one particular market variable (e.g. the price of gold). The chapter covers the approaches used by the trader to manage risk.

The trader must monitor a number of risk measures (known as "Greek letters" or just "Greeks") and try to ensure that they remain within reasonable bounds. The most important Greek letter is delta. This is the rate of change of the value of the trader's portfolio with respect to the market variable. The trader can make delta zero by doing a trade involving the underlying market variable. Suppose for example that the trader responsible for instruments dependent on the price of gold has a portfolio with a delta of $-100,000$ when the price of gold is $1,200 per ounce. This means that the portfolio decreases in value by $100,000 when the price of gold increases from $1,200 to $1,201. Delta can be changed to zero by buying 100,000 ounces of gold. (Make sure you understand why this is so.) A portfolio with a delta of zero is known as a delta-neutral portfolio.

Option traders usually make their portfolios delta neutral (or close to delta neutral) as a matter of course at the end of each day. This is known as rebalancing the portfolio. It makes their portfolios relatively insensitive to small changes in the underlying market variable (the price of gold in our example). Tables 17.2 and 17.3 provide examples of how a trader with a portfolio consisting of a single option might fare if the portfolio is rebalanced, bringing delta to zero, every week. You should study these tables carefully and make sure you understand them. The process of bringing delta to zero at regular intervals is known as delta hedging. It underlies the no arbitrage argument for pricing options.

Delta hedging provides protection against small changes in the underlying variable. Gamma measures a trader's exposure to large jumps. Gamma is defined as the rate of change of delta with respect to the underlying variable. Figure 17.7 illustrates how gamma risk arises. The value of the option is assumed to move from C to C' when delta hedging is used. In fact it moves from C to C''.

Vega measures the sensitivity of a portfolio to changes in volatility. Neither gamma nor vega can be changed by taking a position in the underlying asset. It is necessary to take a position in a derivative such as an option to change these Greek letters. As explained in Business Snapshot 17.1 traders tend to manage gamma and vega opportunistically.

Other Greek letters covered in the chapter are theta (sensitivity to the passage of time) and rho (sensitivity to interest rates).

The last part of the chapter covers portfolio insurance and the creation of options synthetically. When we wish to hedge an option we use a trading strategy that neutralizes delta (as in Tables 17.2 and 17.3). When we wish to create an option synthetically we use a trading strategy that matches the delta of the option we are trying to create. As explained in Section 17.13 the creation of a synthetic put option on a portfolio of stocks involves buying stocks (or index futures) just after a price rise and selling stocks (or index futures) just after a price fall. As traders found in October 1987, if too many portfolio managers are attempting to create put options synthetically at the same time, the strategy may not produce the desired results.

Software

The Equity_FX_Indx_Fut_Calc worksheet of DG400f.xls allows you to calculate Greek letters for European and American options on stocks, foreign exchange, indices, and futures. Application B in DG400f Applications.xls produces charts for Greek letters similar to those that appear in the chapter. Application C in DG400f Applications.xls produces tables similar to Tables 17.2 and 17.3.

Answers to Practice Questions

Problem 17.8.
What does it mean to assert that the theta of an option position is –0.1 when time is measured in years? If a trader feels that neither a stock price nor its implied volatility will change, what type of option position is appropriate?

A theta of -0.1 means that if Δt years pass with no change in either the stock price or its volatility, the value of the option declines by $0.1\Delta t$. A trader who feels that neither the stock price nor its implied volatility will change should write an option to create as high a positive theta position as possible.

Problem 17.9.
The Black–Scholes–Merton price of an out-of-the-money call option with an exercise price of $40 is $4. A trader who has written the option plans to use a stop-loss strategy. The trader's plan is to buy at $40.10 and to sell at $39.90. Estimate the expected number of times the stock will be bought or sold.

The strategy costs the trader 0.10 each time the stock is bought or sold. The total expected cost of the strategy, in present value terms, must be $4. This means that the expected number of times the stock will be bought or sold is approximately 40. The expected number of times it will be bought is approximately 20 and the expected number of times it will be sold is also approximately 20. The buy and sell transactions can take place at any time during the life of the option. The above numbers are therefore only approximately correct because of the effects of discounting. Also the estimate is of the number of times the stock is bought or sold in the risk-neutral world, not the real world.

Problem 17.10.
Suppose that a stock price is currently $20 and that a call option with an exercise price of $25 is created synthetically using a continually changing position in the stock. Consider the following two scenarios:
a) *Stock price increases steadily from $20 to $35 during the life of the option.*
b) *Stock price oscillates wildly, ending up at $35.*
Which scenario would make the synthetically created option more expensive? Explain your

answer.

The holding of the stock at any given time must be $N(d_1)$. Hence the stock is bought just after the price has risen and sold just after the price has fallen. (This is the buy high sell low strategy referred to in the text.) In the first scenario the stock is continually bought. In second scenario the stock is bought, sold, bought again, sold again, etc. The final holding is the same in both scenarios. The buy, sell, buy, sell... situation clearly leads to higher costs than the buy, buy, buy... situation. This problem emphasizes one disadvantage of creating options synthetically. Whereas the cost of an option that is purchased is known up front and depends on the forecasted volatility, the cost of an option that is created synthetically is not known up front and depends on the volatility actually encountered.

Problem 17.11.
What is the delta of a short position in 1,000 European call options on silver futures? The options mature in eight months, and the futures contract underlying the option matures in nine months. The current nine-month futures price is $8 per ounce, the exercise price of the options is $8, the risk-free interest rate is 12% per annum, and the volatility of silver futures prices is 18% per annum.

The delta of a European futures call option is usually defined as the rate of change of the option price with respect to the futures price (not the spot price). It is
$$e^{-rT}N(d_1)$$
In this case $F_0 = 8$, $K = 8$, $r = 0.12$, $\sigma = 0.18$, $T = 0.6667$
$$d_1 = \frac{\ln(8/8) + (0.18^2/2) \times 0.6667}{0.18\sqrt{0.6667}} = 0.0735$$
$N(d_1) = 0.5293$ and the delta of the option is
$$e^{-0.12 \times 0.6667} \times 0.5293 = 0.4886$$
The delta of a short position in 1,000 futures options is therefore -488.6.

Problem 17.12.
In Problem 17.11, what initial position in nine-month silver futures is necessary for delta hedging? If silver itself is used, what is the initial position? If one-year silver futures are used, what is the initial position? Assume no storage costs for silver.

In order to answer this problem it is important to distinguish between the rate of change of the option with respect to the futures price and the rate of change of its price with respect to the spot price.
The former will be referred to as the futures delta; the latter will be referred to as the spot delta. The futures delta of a nine-month futures contract to buy one ounce of silver is by definition 1.0. Hence, from the answer to Problem 17.11, a long position in nine-month futures on 488.6 ounces is necessary to hedge the option position.
The spot delta of a nine-month futures contract is $e^{0.12 \times 0.75} = 1.094$ assuming no storage costs. (This is because silver can be treated in the same way as a non-dividend-paying stock when there are no storage costs. $F_0 = S_0 e^{rT}$ so that the spot delta is the futures delta times e^{rT}.) Hence the

spot delta of the option position is $-488.6 \times 1.094 = -534.6$. Thus a long position in 534.6 ounces of silver is necessary to hedge the option position.

The spot delta of a one-year silver futures contract to buy one ounce of silver is $e^{0.12} = 1.1275$. Hence a long position in $e^{-0.12} \times 534.6 = 474.1$ ounces of one-year silver futures is necessary to hedge the option position.

Problem 17.13.
A company uses delta hedging to hedge a portfolio of long positions in put and call options on a currency. Which of the following would give the most favorable result?
a) *A virtually constant spot rate*
b) *Wild movements in the spot rate*
Explain your answer.

A long position in either a put or a call option has a positive gamma. From Figure 17.8, when gamma is positive the hedger gains from a large change in the stock price and loses from a small change in the stock price. Hence the hedger will fare better in case (b).

Problem 17.14.
Repeat Problem 17.13 for a financial institution with a portfolio of short positions in put and call options on a currency.

A short position in either a put or a call option has a negative gamma. From Figure 17.8, when gamma is negative the hedger gains from a small change in the stock price and loses from a large change in the stock price. Hence the hedger will fare better in case (a).

Problem 17.15.
A financial institution has just sold 1,000 seven-month European call options on the Japanese yen. Suppose that the spot exchange rate is 0.80 cent per yen, the exercise price is 0.81 cent per yen, the risk-free interest rate in the United States is 8% per annum, the risk-free interest rate in Japan is 5% per annum, and the volatility of the yen is 15% per annum. Calculate the delta, gamma, vega, theta, and rho of the financial institution's position. Interpret each number.

In this case $S_0 = 0.80$, $K = 0.81$, $r = 0.08$, $r_f = 0.05$, $\sigma = 0.15$, $T = 0.5833$

$$d_1 = \frac{\ln(0.80/0.81) + \left(0.08 - 0.05 + 0.15^2/2\right) \times 0.5833}{0.15\sqrt{0.5833}} = 0.1016$$

$$d_2 = d_1 - 0.15\sqrt{0.5833} = -0.0130$$

$$N(d_1) = 0.5405; \quad N(d_2) = 0.4998$$

The delta of one call option is $e^{-r_f T} N(d_1) = e^{-0.05 \times 0.5833} \times 0.5405 = 0.5250$.

$$N'(d_1) = \frac{1}{\sqrt{2\pi}} e^{-d_1^2/2} = \frac{1}{\sqrt{2\pi}} e^{-0.00516} = 0.3969$$

so that the gamma of one call option is

$$\frac{N'(d_1)e^{-r_fT}}{S_0\sigma\sqrt{T}} = \frac{0.3969\times0.9713}{0.80\times0.15\times\sqrt{0.5833}} = 4.206$$

The vega of one call option is

$$S_0\sqrt{T}N'(d_1)e^{-r_fT} = 0.80\sqrt{0.5833}\times0.3969\times0.9713 = 0.2355$$

The theta of one call option is

$$-\frac{S_0N'(d_1)\sigma e^{-r_fT}}{2\sqrt{T}} + r_fS_0N(d_1)e^{-r_fT} - rKe^{-rT}N(d_2)$$

$$= -\frac{0.8\times0.3969\times0.15\times0.9713}{2\sqrt{0.5833}}$$

$$+0.05\times0.8\times0.5405\times0.9713 - 0.08\times0.81\times0.9544\times0.4948$$

$$= -0.0399$$

The rho of one call option is

$$KTe^{-rT}N(d_2)$$
$$= 0.81\times0.5833\times0.9544\times0.4948$$
$$= 0.2231$$

Delta can be interpreted as meaning that, when the spot price increases by a small amount (measured in cents), the value of an option to buy one yen increases by 0.525 times that amount. Gamma can be interpreted as meaning that, when the spot price increases by a small amount (measured in cents), the delta increases by 4.206 times that amount. Vega can be interpreted as meaning that, when the volatility (measured in decimal form) increases by a small amount, the option's value increases by 0.2355 times that amount. When volatility increases by 1% (= 0.01) the option price increases by 0.002355. Theta can be interpreted as meaning that, when a small amount of time (measured in years) passes, the option's value decreases by 0.0399 times that amount. In particular when one calendar day passes it decreases by $0.0399/365 = 0.000109$. Finally, rho can be interpreted as meaning that, when the interest rate (measured in decimal form) increases by a small amount the option's value increases by 0.2231 times that amount. When the interest rate increases by 1% (= 0.01), the options value increases by 0.002231.

Problem 17.16.
Under what circumstances is it possible to make a European option on a stock index both gamma neutral and vega neutral by adding a position in one other European option?

Assume that S_0, K, r, σ, T, q are the parameters for the option held and S_0, K^*, r, σ, T^*, q are the parameters for another option. Suppose that d_1 has its usual meaning and is calculated on the basis of the first set of parameters while d_1^* is the value of d_1 calculated on the basis of the second set of parameters. Suppose further that w of the second option are held for each of the first option held. The gamma of the portfolio is:

$$\alpha\left[\frac{N'(d_1)e^{-qT}}{S_0\sigma\sqrt{T}} + w\frac{N'(d_1^*)e^{-qT^*}}{S_0\sigma\sqrt{T^*}}\right]$$

where α is the number of the first option held.

Since we require gamma to be zero:

$$w = -\frac{N'(d_1)e^{-q(T-T^*)}}{N'(d_1^*)}\sqrt{\frac{T^*}{T}}$$

The vega of the portfolio is:

$$\alpha\left[S_0\sqrt{T}N'(d_1)e^{-q(T)} + wS_0\sqrt{T^*}N'(d_1^*)e^{-q(T^*)}\right]$$

Since we require vega to be zero:

$$w = -\sqrt{\frac{T}{T^*}}\frac{N'(d_1)e^{-q(T-T^*)}}{N'(d_1^*)}$$

Equating the two expressions for w

$$T^* = T$$

Hence the maturity of the option held must equal the maturity of the option used for hedging.

Problem 17.17.

A fund manager has a well-diversified portfolio that mirrors the performance of the S&P 500 and is worth \$360 million. The value of the S&P 500 is 1,200, and the portfolio manager would like to buy insurance against a reduction of more than 5% in the value of the portfolio over the next six months. The risk-free interest rate is 6% per annum. The dividend yield on both the portfolio and the S&P 500 is 3%, and the volatility of the index is 30% per annum.

a) *If the fund manager buys traded European put options, how much would the insurance cost?*

b) *Explain carefully alternative strategies open to the fund manager involving traded European call options, and show that they lead to the same result.*

c) *If the fund manager decides to provide insurance by keeping part of the portfolio in risk-free securities, what should the initial position be?*

d) *If the fund manager decides to provide insurance by using nine-month index futures, what should the initial position be?*

The fund is worth \$300,000 times the value of the index. When the value of the portfolio falls by 5% (to \$342 million), the value of the S&P 500 also falls by 5% to 1140. The fund manager therefore requires European put options on 300,000 times the S&P 500 with exercise price 1140.

a) $S_0 = 1200$, $K = 1140$, $r = 0.06$, $\sigma = 0.30$, $T = 0.50$ and $q = 0.03$. Hence:

$$d_1 = \frac{\ln(1200/1140) + (0.06 - 0.03 + 0.3^2/2) \times 0.5}{0.3\sqrt{0.5}} = 0.4186$$

$$d_2 = d_1 - 0.3\sqrt{0.5} = 0.2064$$

$$N(d_1) = 0.6622; \quad N(d_2) = 0.5818$$

$$N(-d_1) = 0.3378; \quad N(-d_2) = 0.4182$$

The value of one put option is

$$1140e^{-rT}N(-d_2)-1200e^{-qT}N(-d_1)$$
$$=1140e^{-0.06\times0.5}\times0.4182-1200e^{-0.03\times0.5}\times0.3378$$
$$=63.40$$

The total cost of the insurance is therefore
$$300,000\times63.40=\$19,020,000$$

b) From put–call parity
$$S_0e^{-qT}+p=c+Ke^{-rT}$$

or:
$$p=c-S_0e^{-qT}+Ke^{-rT}$$

This shows that a put option can be created by selling (or shorting) e^{-qT} of the index, buying a call option and investing the remainder at the risk-free rate of interest. Applying this to the situation under consideration, the fund manager should:
1. Sell $360e^{-0.03\times0.5}$=\$354.64 million of stock
2. Buy call options on 300,000 times the S&P 500 with exercise price 1140 and maturity in six months.
3. Invest the remaining cash at the risk-free interest rate of 6% per annum.
This strategy gives the same result as buying put options directly.

c) The delta of one put option is
$$e^{-qT}[N(d_1)-1]$$
$$=e^{-0.03\times0.5}(0.6622-1)$$
$$-0.3327$$

This indicates that 33.27% of the portfolio (i.e., \$119.77 million) should be initially sold and invested in risk-free securities.

d) The delta of a nine-month index futures contract is
$$e^{(r-q)T}=e^{0.03\times0.75}=1.023$$

The spot short position required is
$$\frac{119,770,000}{1200}=99,808$$

times the index. Hence a short position in
$$\frac{99,808}{1.023\times250}=390$$

futures contracts is required.

Problem 17.18.
Repeat Problem 17.17 on the assumption that the portfolio has a beta of 1.5. Assume that the dividend yield on the portfolio is 4% per annum.

When the value of the portfolio goes down 5% in six months, the total return from the portfolio, including dividends, in the six months is
$$-5+2=-3\%$$
i.e., -6% per annum. This is 12% per annum less than the risk-free interest rate. Since the portfolio has a beta of 1.5 we would expect the market to provide a return of 8% per annum less than the risk-free interest rate, i.e., we would expect the market to provide a return of -2% per annum. Since dividends on the market index are 3% per annum, we would expect the market index to have dropped at the rate of 5% per annum or 2.5% per six months; i.e., we would expect the market to have dropped to 1170. A total of $450,000 = (1.5 \times 300,000)$ put options on the S&P 500 with exercise price 1170 and exercise date in six months are therefore required.

a) $S_0 = 1200$, $K = 1170$, $r = 0.06$, $\sigma = 0.3$, $T = 0.5$ and $q = 0.03$. Hence
$$d_1 = \frac{\ln(1200/1170) + (0.06 - 0.03 + 0.09/2) \times 0.5}{0.3\sqrt{0.5}} = 0.2961$$

$$d_2 = d_1 - 0.3\sqrt{0.5} = 0.0840$$
$$N(d_1) = 0.6164; \quad N(d_2) = 0.5335$$
$$N(-d_1) = 0.3836; \quad N(-d_2) = 0.4665$$

The value of one put option is
$$Ke^{-rT}N(-d_2) - S_0e^{-qT}N(-d_1)$$
$$= 1170e^{-0.06 \times 0.5} \times 0.4665 - 1200e^{-0.03 \times 0.5} \times 0.3836$$
$$= 76.28$$

The total cost of the insurance is therefore
$$450,000 \times 76.28 = \$34,326,000$$

Note that this is much greater than the cost of the insurance in Problem 17.17.

b) As in Problem 17.17 the fund manager can 1) sell $354.64 million of stock, 2) buy call options on 450,000 times the S&P 500 with exercise price 1170 and exercise date in six months and 3) invest the remaining cash at the risk-free interest rate.

c) The portfolio is 50% more volatile than the S&P 500. When the insurance is considered as an option on the portfolio the parameters are as follows: $S_0 = 360$, $K = 342$, $r = 0.06$, $\sigma = 0.45$, $T = 0.5$ and $q = 0.04$

$$d_1 = \frac{\ln(360/342) + \left(0.06 - 0.04 + 0.45^2/2\right) \times 0.5}{0.45\sqrt{0.5}} = 0.3517$$

$$N(d_1) = 0.6374$$

The delta of the option is

$$e^{-qT}[N(d_1) - 1]$$
$$= e^{-0.04 \times 0.5}(0.6374 - 1)$$
$$= -0.355$$

This indicates that 35.5% of the portfolio (i.e., \$127.8 million) should be sold and invested in riskless securities.

d) We now return to the situation considered in (a) where put options on the index are required. The delta of each put option is

$$e^{-qT}(N(d_1) - 1)$$
$$= e^{-0.03 \times 0.5}(0.6164 - 1)$$
$$= -0.3779$$

The delta of the total position required in put options is $-450,000 \times 0.3779 = -170,000$. The delta of a nine month index futures is (see Problem 17.17) 1,023. Hence a short position in

$$\frac{170,000}{1.023 \times 250} = 665$$

index futures contracts is required.

Problem 17.19.

Show by substituting for the various terms in equation (17.4) that the equation is true for:
   a) *A single European call option on a non-dividend-paying stock*
   b) *A single European put option on a non-dividend-paying stock*
   c) *Any portfolio of European put and call options on a non-dividend-paying stock*

a) For a call option on a non-dividend-paying stock

$$\Delta = N(d_1)$$

$$\Gamma = \frac{N'(d_1)}{S_0 \sigma \sqrt{T}}$$

$$\Theta = -\frac{S_0 N'(d_1)\sigma}{2\sqrt{T}} - rKe^{-rT}N(d_2)$$

Hence the left-hand side of equation (17.4) is:

$$= -\frac{S_0 N'(d_1)\sigma}{2\sqrt{T}} - rKe^{-rT}N(d_2) + rS_0 N(d_1) + \frac{1}{2}\sigma S_0 \frac{N'(d_1)}{\sqrt{T}}$$

$$= r[S_0 N(d_1) - Ke^{-rT}N(d_2)]$$

$$= r\Pi$$

b) For a put option on a non-dividend-paying stock

$$\Delta = N(d_1) - 1 = -N(-d_1)$$

$$\Gamma = \frac{N'(d_1)}{S_0 \sigma \sqrt{T}}$$

$$\Theta = -\frac{S_0 N'(d_1)\sigma}{2\sqrt{T}} + rKe^{-rT}N(-d_2)$$

Hence the left-hand side of equation (17.4) is:

$$-\frac{S_0 N'(d_1)\sigma}{2\sqrt{T}} + rKe^{-rT}N(-d_2) - rS_0 N(-d_1) + \frac{1}{2}\sigma S_0 \frac{N'(d_1)}{\sqrt{T}}$$

$$= r[Ke^{-rT}N(-d_2) - S_0 N(-d_1)]$$

$$= r\Pi$$

c) For a portfolio of options, Π, Δ, Θ and Γ are the sums of their values for the individual options in the portfolio. It follows that equation (17.4) is true for any portfolio of European put and call options.

Problem 17.20.

Suppose that $70 billion of equity assets are the subject of portfolio insurance schemes. Assume that the schemes are designed to provide insurance against the value of the assets declining by more than 5% within one year. Making whatever estimates you find necessary, use the DerivaGem software to calculate the value of the stock or futures contracts that the administrators of the portfolio insurance schemes will attempt to sell if the market falls by 23% in a single day.

We can regard the position of all portfolio insurers taken together as a single put option. The three known parameters of the option, before the 23% decline, are $S_0 = 70$, $K = 66.5$, $T = 1$.
Other parameters can be estimated as $r = 0.06$, $\sigma = 0.25$ and $q = 0.03$. Then:

$$d_1 = \frac{\ln(70/66.5) + (0.06 - 0.03 + 0.25^2/2)}{0.25} = 0.4502$$

$$N(d_1) = 0.6737$$

The delta of the option is

$$e^{-qT}[N(d_1) - 1]$$

$$= e^{-0.03}(0.6737 - 1)$$

$$= -0.3167$$

117

This shows that 31.67% or $22.17 billion of assets should have been sold before the decline. These numbers can also be produced from DG400f.xls by selecting Underlying Type in the first worksheet as Index and Option Type as Analytic European.

After the decline, $S_0 = 53.9$, $K = 66.5$, $T = 1$, $r = 0.06$, $\sigma = 0.25$ and $q = 0.03$.

$$d_1 = \frac{\ln(53.9/66.5) + (0.06 - 0.03 + 0.25^2/2)}{0.25} = -0.5953$$

and $N(d_1) = 0.2758$. The delta of the option has dropped to

$$e^{-0.03 \times 0.5}(0.2758 - 1)$$

$$= -0.7028$$

This shows that cumulatively 70.28% of the assets originally held should be sold. An additional 38.61% of the original portfolio should be sold. The sales measured at pre-crash prices are about $27.0 billion. At post-crash prices they are about 20.8 billion.

Problem 17.21.
Does a forward contract on a stock index have the same delta as the corresponding futures contract? Explain your answer.

With our usual notation the value of a forward contract on the asset is $S_0 e^{-qT} - Ke^{-rT}$. When there is a small change, ΔS, in S_0 the value of the forward contract changes by $e^{-qT}\Delta S$. The delta of the forward contract is therefore e^{-qT}. The futures price is $S_0 e^{(r-q)T}$. When there is a small change, ΔS, in S_0 the futures price changes by $\Delta S e^{(r-q)T}$. Given the daily settlement procedures in futures contracts, this is also the immediate change in the wealth of the holder of the futures contract. The delta of the futures contract is therefore $e^{(r-q)T}$. We conclude that the deltas of a futures and forward contract are not the same. The delta of the futures is greater than the delta of the corresponding forward by a factor of e^{rT}.

Problem 17.22.
A bank's position in options on the dollar–euro exchange rate has a delta of 30,000 and a gamma of $-80,000$. Explain how these numbers can be interpreted. The exchange rate (dollars per euro) is 0.90. What position would you take to make the position delta neutral? After a short period of time, the exchange rate moves to 0.93. Estimate the new delta. What additional trade is necessary to keep the position delta neutral? Assuming the bank did set up a delta-neutral position originally, has it gained or lost money from the exchange-rate movement?

The delta indicates that when the value of the euro exchange rate increases by $0.01, the value of the bank's position increases by $0.01 \times 30,000 = \$300$. The gamma indicates that when the euro exchange rate increases by $0.01 the delta of the portfolio decreases by $0.01 \times 80,000 = 800$. For delta neutrality 30,000 euros should be shorted. When the exchange rate moves up to 0.93, we expect the delta of the portfolio to decrease by $(0.93 - 0.90) \times 80,000 = 2,400$ so that it becomes 27,600. To maintain delta neutrality, it is therefore necessary for the bank to unwind its short position 2,400 euros so that a net 27,600 have been shorted. As shown in the text (see Figure 17.8), when a portfolio is delta neutral and has a negative gamma, a loss is experienced when there is a large movement in the underlying asset price. We can conclude that the bank is likely to have lost money.

CHAPTER 18
Binomial Trees in Practice

This chapter provides more detail on the use of binomial trees than Chapter 12. It starts by explaining where the formulas for u, d, and p come from. When the length of the time step is Δt, the formulas ensure that
1. The expected return on the stock in time Δt is the risk-free rate, r.
2. The standard deviation of the return in time Δt is $\sigma\sqrt{\Delta t}$ where σ is the volatility

Make sure you understand the calculations in Figure 18.3.

The chapter shows how the Greek letters discussed in Chapter 17 can be calculated. For delta we look at the two nodes at time Δt. We calculate the change in the option price when we move from the lower node to the upper node and the change in the stock price when we do so. Delta is the ratio of the option price change to the stock price change. Gamma is calculated from the three nodes at time $2\Delta t$. The upper two nodes produce one delta estimate and the lower two nodes produce another delta estimate. These two estimates of delta can be used to provide an estimate of gamma. Theta can be calculated from the tree by comparing option prices at time zero with the option price at the middle node at time $2\Delta t$. Vega is calculated by making a small change to the volatility, re-computing the tree, and observing the option value calculated.

An important issue for stock options is how to deal with dividends. On approach is to assume a known dividend yield (i.e., to assume that the dividend as a percent of the stock price is known). This is fairly straightforward. In many instances it is more accurate to assume the cash amount of the dividend is known. As indicated in Figure 18.6, the tree does not naturally recombine when this assumption is made. An approach that ensures a recombining tree involves the following two stages:
1. Build a tree for the stock price less the present value of future dividends during the life of the option; and
2. Add the present value of future dividends at each node to construct the final tree.

In Example 18.3, the first stage results in the tree in Figure 18.3. The second stage results in the tree attached to the Example.

Sections 18.4 and 18.5 discuss a number of extensions of the basic tree-building approach. They show that:
1. We can make the short-term interest rate a function of time by making the probability of an up movement a function of time.
2. We can make volatility a function of time by having non-equal time steps.
3. We can improve accuracy by using the same tree to value both an American option and the corresponding European option. The error in the price of the European option is assumed to be the same as that of the American option. (This is known as the control variate technique.)
4. Instead of setting $d = 1/u$ we can choose the geometry of the tree so that $p = 0.5$ (see Section 18.5).

Section 18.6 points out that instead of working back from the end of the tree to the beginning, we can use Monte Carlo simulation to sample paths starting at the beginning of the tree. Study the example in Section 18.6 to make sure you understand how to use this technique to price path-dependent options.

Software

The Equity_FX_Indx_Fut_Calc worksheet of DG400f.xls allows you to value options using binomial trees and to display the trees that are produced. Choose as the Option Type *Binomial: European* or *Binomial American* and indicate in *Tree Steps* the number of steps you want to use on the tree. Once you have calculated the price of an option you can click on a box to display the tree and see the calculations that have been carried out. If you specify more than 10 tree steps the tree displayed is the one that would be used if 10 tree steps had been specified.

Answers to Practice Questions

Problem 18.8.
Consider an option that pays off the amount by which the final stock price exceeds the average stock price achieved during the life of the option. Can this be valued from a binomial tree using backwards induction?

No! This is an example of a *path-dependent option*. The payoff depends on the path followed by the stock price as well as on its final value. The option cannot be valued by starting at the end of the tree and working backward, because the payoff at a final branch depends on the path used to reach it. European options for which the payoff depends on the average stock price can be valued using Monte Carlo simulation, as described in Section 18.6.

Problem 18.9.
A nine-month American put option on a non-dividend-paying stock has a strike price of $49. The stock price is $50, the risk-free rate is 5% per annum, and the volatility is 30% per annum. Use a three-step binomial tree to calculate the option price.

In this case, $S_0 = 50$, $K = 49$, $r = 0.05$, $\sigma = 0.30$, $T = 0.75$, and $\Delta t = 0.25$. Also

$$u = e^{\sigma\sqrt{\Delta t}} = e^{0.30\sqrt{0.25}} = 1.1618$$

$$d = \frac{1}{u} = 0.8607$$

$$a = e^{r\Delta t} = e^{0.05 \times 0.25} = 1.0126$$

$$p = \frac{a - d}{u - d} = 0.5043$$

$$1 - p = 0.4957$$

The output from DerivaGem for this example is shown in the Figure S18.1. The calculated price of the option is $4.29. Using 100 steps the price obtained is $3.91.

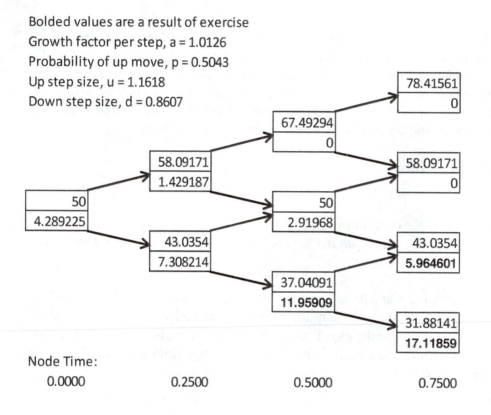

Bolded values are a result of exercise
Growth factor per step, a = 1.0126
Probability of up move, p = 0.5043
Up step size, u = 1.1618
Down step size, d = 0.8607

Node Time:
0.0000   0.2500   0.5000   0.7500

Figure S18.1   Tree for Problem 18.9

Problem 18.10.

Use a three-time-step tree to value a nine-month American call option on wheat futures. The current futures price is 400 cents, the strike price is 420 cents, the risk-free rate is 6%, and the volatility is 35% per annum. Estimate the delta of the option from your tree.

In this case $F_0 = 400$, $K = 420$, $r = 0.06$, $\sigma = 0.35$, $T = 0.75$, and $\Delta t = 0.25$. Also

$$u = e^{0.35\sqrt{0.25}} = 1.1912$$

$$d = \frac{1}{u} = 0.8395$$

$$a = 1$$

$$p = \frac{a-d}{u-d} = 0.4564$$

$$1 - p = 0.5436$$

The output from DerivaGem for this example is shown in the Figure S18.2. The calculated price

122

of the option is 42.07 cents. Using 100 time steps the price obtained is 38.64. The option's delta is calculated from the tree is
$$(79.971 - 11.419) / (476.498 - 335.783) = 0.487$$
When 100 steps are used the estimate of the option's delta is 0.483.

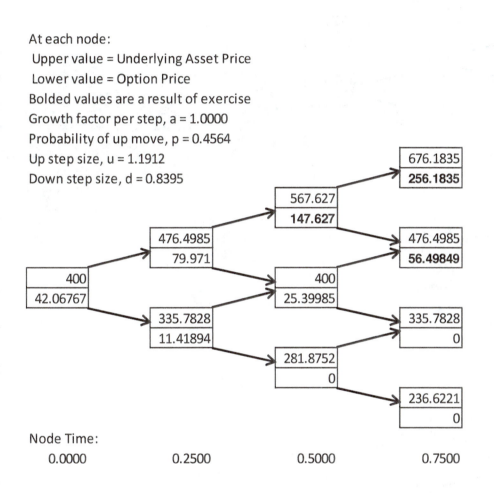

At each node:
Upper value = Underlying Asset Price
Lower value = Option Price
Bolded values are a result of exercise
Growth factor per step, a = 1.0000
Probability of up move, p = 0.4564
Up step size, u = 1.1912
Down step size, d = 0.8395

Node Time:
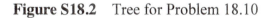
0.0000   0.2500   0.5000   0.7500

Figure S18.2   Tree for Problem 18.10

Problem 18.11.
A three-month American call option on a stock has a strike price of $20. The stock price is $20, the risk-free rate is 3% per annum, and the volatility is 25% per annum. A dividend of $2 is expected in 1.5 months. Use a three-step binomial tree to calculate the option price.

In this case the present value of the dividend is $2e^{-0.03 \times 0.125} = 1.9925$. We first build a tree for $S_0 = 20 - 1.9925 = 18.0075$, $K = 20$, $r = 0.03$, $\sigma = 0.25$, and $T = 0.25$ with $\Delta t = 0.08333$. This gives Figure S18.3. For nodes between times0 and 1.5 months we then add the present value of the dividend to the stock price. The result is the tree in Figure S18.4. The price of the option calculated from the tree is 0.674. When 100 steps are used the price obtained is 0.690.

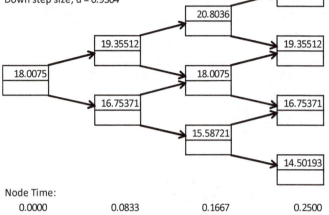

Tree shows stock prices less PV of dividend at 0.125 years
Growth factor per step, a = 1.0025
Probability of up move, p = 0.4993
Up step size, u = 1.0748
Down step size, d = 0.9304

22.36047

20.8036

19.35512   19.35512

18.0075   18.0075

16.75371

16.75371

15.58721

14.50193

Node Time:
0.0000   0.0833   0.1667   0.2500

Figure S18.3   First tree for Problem 18.11

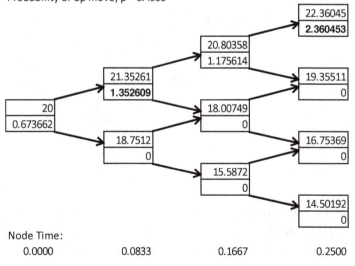

At each node:
 Upper value = Underlying Asset Price
 Lower value = Option Price
 Bolded values are a result of exercise
 Probability of up move, p = 0.4993

22.36045
2.360453

20.80358
1.175614

21.35261
1.352609

19.35511
0

20   18.00749
0.673662   0

18.7512
0

16.75369
0

15.5872
0

14.50192
0

Node Time:
0.0000   0.0833   0.1667   0.2500

Figure S18.4   Final Tree for Problem 18.11

124

Problem 18.12.

A one-year American put option on a non-dividend-paying stock has an exercise price of $18. The current stock price is $20, the risk-free interest rate is 15% per annum, and the volatility of the stock is 40% per annum. Use the DerivaGem software with four three-month time steps to estimate the value of the option. Display the tree and verify that the option prices at the final and penultimate nodes are correct. Use DerivaGem to value the European version of the option. Use the control variate technique to improve your estimate of the price of the American option.

In this case $S_0 = 20$, $K = 18$, $r = 0.15$, $\sigma = 0.40$, $T = 1$, and $\Delta t = 0.25$. The parameters for the tree are

$$u = e^{\sigma\sqrt{\Delta t}} = e^{0.4\sqrt{0.25}} = 1.2214$$

$$d = 1/u = 0.8187$$

$$a = e^{r\Delta t} = 1.0382$$

$$p = \frac{a-d}{u-d} = \frac{1.0382 - 0.8187}{1.2214 - 0.8187} = 0.545$$

The tree produced by DerivaGem for the American option is shown in Figure S18.5. The estimated value of the American option is $1.29.

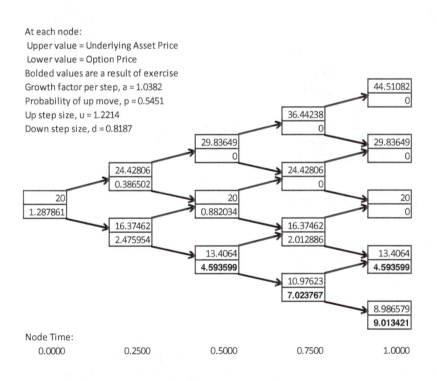

At each node:
Upper value = Underlying Asset Price
Lower value = Option Price
Bolded values are a result of exercise
Growth factor per step, a = 1.0382
Probability of up move, p = 0.5451
Up step size, u = 1.2214
Down step size, d = 0.8187

Node Time:
0.0000   0.2500   0.5000   0.7500   1.0000

Figure S18.5   Tree to evaluate American option for Problem 18.12

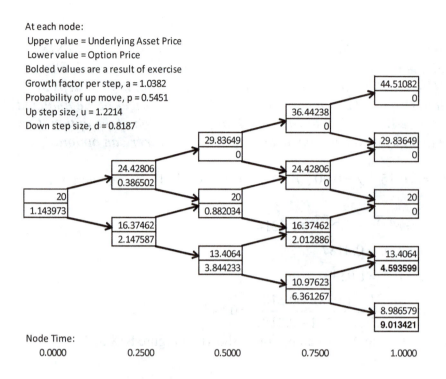

At each node:
Upper value = Underlying Asset Price
Lower value = Option Price
Bolded values are a result of exercise
Growth factor per step, a = 1.0382
Probability of up move, p = 0.5451
Up step size, u = 1.2214
Down step size, d = 0.8187

Node Time:
0.0000　　0.2500　　0.5000　　0.7500　　1.0000

Figure S18.6　Tree to evaluate European option in Problem 18.12

As shown in Figure S18.6, the same tree can be used to value a European put option with the same parameters. The estimated value of the European option is \$1.14. The option parameters are $S_0 = 20$, $K = 18$, $r = 0.15$, $\sigma = 0.40$ and $T = 1$

$$d_1 = \frac{\ln(20/18) + 0.15 + 0.40^2/2}{0.40} = 0.8384$$

$$d_2 = d_1 - 0.40 = 0.4384$$

$$N(-d_1) = 0.2009; \quad N(-d_2) = 0.3306$$

The true European put price is therefore

$$18e^{-0.15} \times 0.3306 - 20 \times 0.2009 = 1.10$$

This can also be obtained from DerivaGem. The control variate estimate of the American put price is therefore $1.29 + 1.10 - 1.14 = \$1.25$.

Problem 18.13.

A two-month American put option on a stock index has an exercise price of 480. The current level of the index is 484, the risk-free interest rate is 10% per annum, the dividend yield on the index is 3% per annum, and the volatility of the index is 25% per annum. Divide the life of the option into four half-month periods and use the binomial tree approach to estimate the value of the option.

In this case $S_0 = 484$, $K = 480$, $r = 0.10$, $\sigma = 0.25$ $q = 0.03$, $T = 0.1667$, and $\Delta t = 0.04167$

$$u = e^{\sigma\sqrt{\Delta t}} = e^{0.25\sqrt{0.04167}} = 1.0524$$

$$d = \frac{1}{u} = 0.9502$$

$$a = e^{(r-q)\Delta t} = 1.00292$$

$$p = \frac{a-d}{u-d} = \frac{1.0029-0.9502}{1.0524-0.9502} = 0.516$$

The tree produced by DerivaGem is shown in the Figure S18.7. The estimated price of the option is $14.93.

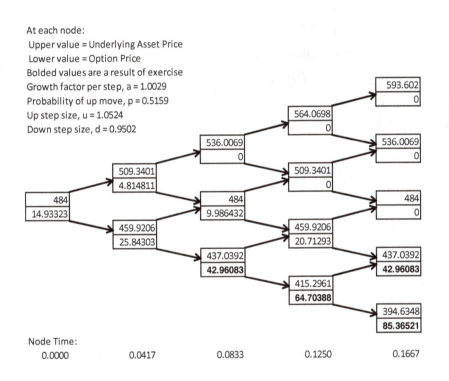

At each node:
Upper value = Underlying Asset Price
Lower value = Option Price
Bolded values are a result of exercise
Growth factor per step, a = 1.0029
Probability of up move, p = 0.5159
Up step size, u = 1.0524
Down step size, d = 0.9502

Node Time:
0.0000   0.0417   0.0833   0.1250   0.1667

Figure S18.7   Tree to evaluate option in Problem 18.13

Problem 18.14.

How would you use the control variate approach to improve the estimate of the delta of an American option when the binomial tree approach is used?

First the delta of the American option is estimated in the usual way from the tree. Denote this by Δ_A^*. Then the delta of a European option which has the same parameters as the American option is calculated in the same way using the same tree. Denote this by Δ_B^*. Finally the true European delta, Δ_B, is calculated using the formulas in Chapter 17. The control variate estimate of delta is then:

$$\Delta_A^* - \Delta_B^* + \Delta_B$$

Problem 18.15.
How would you use the binomial tree approach to value an American option on a stock index when the dividend yield on the index is a function of time?

When the dividend yield is constant

$$u = e^{\sigma\sqrt{\Delta t}}$$

$$d = \frac{1}{u}$$

$$p = \frac{a-d}{u-d}$$

$$a = e^{(r-q)\Delta t}$$

Making the dividend yield, q, a function of time makes a, and therefore p, a function of time. However, it does not affect u or d. It follows that if q is a function of time we can use the same tree by making the probabilities a function of time. The interest rate r can also be a function of time as described in Section 18.4.

CHAPTER 19
Volatility Smiles

The Black-Scholes-Merton model and binomial trees assume that the probability distribution of the underlying asset at a future time is lognormal. If traders wanted to make that assumption they would use the same volatility to price options with different strike prices. In practice the implied volatility of an option is a function of the strike price. Figure 19.1 shows the typical situation for options on a foreign currency (The relationship between implied volatility and strike price is U-shaped). Figure 19.2 shows the future probability distribution for an exchange rate that is consistent with the implied volatilities that traders are using for foreign currency options. It has heavier right and left tails than the lognormal distribution. Figure 19.3 shows the typical situation for options on stocks and stock indices. (The implied volatility is a declining function of strike price.) Figure 19.4 shows the future probability distribution that is consistent with the implied volatilities that traders are using for stocks and stock indices. It has a heavier left tail and a less heavy right tail than the lognormal distribution.

Note that we do not have to worry about whether we are talking about put or call options when constructing diagrams such as Figure 19.1 and 19.3. This is because put-call parity shows that the implied volatility of a European put should be the same as that of a European call (see the appendix to Chapter 19). The same is usually approximately true of American options.

The volatility smile for options on foreign currencies in Figure 19.1 is likely a result of jumps and the fact that volatility is not constant. The volatility smile for options on equities in Figure 19.3 can be explained by the impact of leverage. (As the stock price declines the company becomes more highly levered and volatility increases.) Another possible explanation is "crashophobia." Since 1987 traders have been very concerned about the possibility of another stock market crash and have as a result increased the prices of deep-out-of-the-money put options.

The implied volatilities from the original Black-Scholes-Merton model and its extensions are often used to communicate the prices of European and American call and put options. Traders use a volatility surface such that shown in Table 19.2 when trading options. The volatility surface is an interpolation tool enabling them to estimate the appropriate implied volatility for any standard option trade that is proposed.

Answers to Practice Questions

Problem 19.8.
A stock price is currently $20. Tomorrow, news is expected to be announced that will either increase the price by $5 or decrease the price by $5. What are the problems in using Black–Scholes to value one-month options on the stock?

The probability distribution of the stock price in one month is not lognormal. Possibly it consists of two lognormal distributions superimposed upon each other and is bimodal. Black–Scholes–Merton is clearly inappropriate, because it assumes that the stock price at any future time is lognormal.

Problem 19.9.

What volatility smile is likely to be observed for six-month options when the volatility is uncertain and positively correlated to the stock price?

When the asset price is positively correlated with volatility, the volatility tends to increase as the asset price increases, producing less heavy left tails and heavier right tails. Implied volatility then increases with the strike price.

Problem 19.10.

What problems do you think would be encountered in testing a stock option pricing model empirically?

There are a number of problems in testing an option pricing model empirically. These include the problem of obtaining synchronous data on stock prices and option prices, the problem of estimating the dividends that will be paid on the stock during the option's life, the problem of distinguishing between situations where the market is inefficient and situations where the option pricing model is incorrect, and the problems of estimating stock price volatility.

Problem 19.11.

Suppose that a central bank's policy is to allow an exchange rate to fluctuate between 0.97 and 1.03. What pattern of implied volatilities for options on the exchange rate would you expect to see?

In this case the probability distribution of the exchange rate has a thin left tail and a thin right tail relative to the lognormal distribution. We are in the opposite situation to that described for foreign currencies in Section 19.1. Both out-of-the-money and in-the-money calls and puts can be expected to have lower implied volatilities than at-the-money calls and puts. The pattern of implied volatilities is likely to be similar to Figure 19.7.

Problem 19.12.

Option traders sometimes refer to deep-out-of-the-money options as being options on volatility. Why do you think they do this?

A deep-out-of-the-money option has a low value. Decreases in its volatility reduce its value. However, this reduction is small because the value can never go below zero. Increases in its volatility, on the other hand, can lead to significant percentage increases in the value of the option. The option does, therefore, have some of the same attributes as an option on volatility.

Problem 19.13.

A European call option on a certain stock has a strike price of $30, a time to maturity of one year, and an implied volatility of 30%. A European put option on the same stock has a strike price of $30, a time to maturity of one year, and an implied volatility of 33%. What is the arbitrage opportunity open to a trader? Does the arbitrage work only when the lognormal assumption underlying Black–Scholes–Merton holds? Explain the reasons for your answer carefully.

As explained in the appendix to the chapter, put–call parity implies that European put and call options have the same implied volatility. If a call option has an implied volatility of 30% and a put option has an implied volatility of 33%, the call is priced too low relative to the put. The correct trading strategy is to buy the call, sell the put and short the stock. This does not depend on the lognormal assumption underlying Black–Scholes–Merton. Put–call parity is true for any set of assumptions.

Problem 19.14.
Suppose that the result of a major lawsuit affecting a company is due to be announced tomorrow. The company's stock price is currently $60. If the ruling is favorable to the company, the stock price is expected to jump to $75. If it is unfavorable, the stock is expected to jump to $50. What is the risk-neutral probability of a favorable ruling? Assume that the volatility of the company's stock will be 25% for six months after the ruling if the ruling is favorable and 40% if it is unfavorable. Use DerivaGem to calculate the relationship between implied volatility and strike price for six-month European options on the company today. The company does not pay dividends. Assume that the six-month risk-free rate is 6%. Consider call options with strike prices of $30, $40, $50, $60, $70, and $80.

Suppose that p is the probability of a favorable ruling. The expected price of the company's stock tomorrow is

$$75p + 50(1 - p) = 50 + 25p$$

This must be the price of the stock today. (We ignore the expected return to an investor over one day.) Hence

$$50 + 25p = 60$$

or $p = 0.4$.

If the ruling is favorable, the volatility, σ, will be 25%. Other option parameters are $S_0 = 75$, $r = 0.06$, and $T = 0.5$. For a value of K equal to 50, DerivaGem gives the value of a European call option price as 26.502.

If the ruling is unfavorable, the volatility, σ will be 40% Other option parameters are $S_0 = 50$, $r = 0.06$, and $T = 0.5$. For a value of K equal to 50, DerivaGem gives the value of a European call option price as 6.310.

The value today of a European call option with a strike price today is the weighted average of 26.502 and 6.310 or:

$$0.4 \times 26.502 + 0.6 \times 6.310 = 14.387$$

DerivaGem can be used to calculate the implied volatility when the option has this price. The parameter values are $S_0 = 60$, $K = 50$, $T = 0.5$, $r = 0.06$ and $c = 14.387$. The implied volatility is 47.76%.

These calculations can be repeated for other strike prices. The results are shown in the table that follows. The pattern of implied volatilities is shown in Figure S19.1.

131

Strike Price	Call Price: Favorable Outcome	Call Price: Unfavorable Outcome	Weighted Price	Implied Volatility (%)
30	45.887	21.001	30.955	46.67
40	36.182	12.437	21.935	47.78
50	26.502	6.310	14.387	47.76
60	17.171	2.826	8.564	46.05
70	9.334	1.161	4.430	43.22
80	4.159	0.451	1.934	40.36

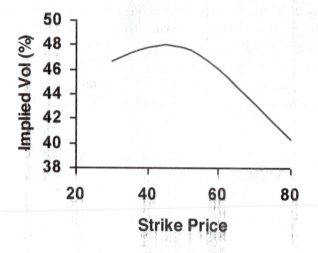

Figure S19.1   Implied Volatilities in Problem 19.14

Problem 19.15.

An exchange rate is currently 0.8000. The volatility of the exchange rate is quoted as 12% and interest rates in the two countries are the same. Using the lognormal assumption, estimate the probability that the exchange rate in three months will be (a) less than 0.7000, (b) between 0.7000 and 0.7500, (c) between 0.7500 and 0.8000, (d) between 0.8000 and 0.8500, (e) between 0.8500 and 0.9000, and (f) greater than 0.9000. Based on the volatility smile usually observed in the market for exchange rates, which of these estimates would you expect to be too low and which would you expect to be too high?

As pointed out in Chapters 5 and 15 an exchange rate behaves like a stock that provides a dividend yield equal to the foreign risk-free rate. Whereas the growth rate in a non-dividend-paying stock in a risk-neutral world is r, the growth rate in the exchange rate in a risk-neutral world is $r - r_f$. Exchange rates have low systematic risks and so we can reasonably assume that this is also the growth rate in the real world. In this case the foreign risk-free rate equals the domestic risk-free rate ($r = r_f$). The expected growth rate in the exchange rate is therefore zero. If S_T is the exchange rate at time T, the probability distribution of $\ln S_T$ is given by equation (13.2) with $\mu = 0$ as

$$\phi\left(\ln S_0 - \sigma^2 T/2, \sigma^2 T\right)$$

where S_0 is the exchange rate at time zero and σ is the volatility of the exchange rate. In this case $S_0 = 0.8000$ and $\sigma = 0.12$, and $T = 0.25$ so that the distribution becomes

$$\phi\left(\ln 0.8 - 0.12^2 \times 0.25/2, \ 0.12^2 \times 0.25\right)$$

or

$$\phi(-0.2249, \ 0.06^2)$$

a) $\ln 0.70 = -0.3567$. The probability that $S_T < 0.70$ is the same as the probability that $\ln S_T < -0.3567$. It is

$$N\left(\frac{-0.3567 + 0.2249}{0.06}\right) = N(-2.1955)$$

This is 1.41%.

b) $\ln 0.75 = -0.2877$. The probability that $S_T < 0.75$ is the same as the probability that $\ln S_T < -0.2877$. It is

$$N\left(\frac{-0.2877 + 0.2249}{0.06}\right) = N(-1.0456)$$

This is 14.79%. The probability that the exchange rate is between 0.70 and 0.75 is therefore $14.79 - 1.41 = 13.38\%$.

c) $\ln 0.80 = -0.2231$. The probability that $S_T < 0.80$ is the same as the probability that $\ln S_T < -0.2231$. It is

$$N\left(\frac{-0.2231 + 0.2249}{0.06}\right) = N(0.0300)$$

This is 51.20%. The probability that the exchange rate is between 0.75 and 0.80 is therefore $51.20 - 14.79 = 36.41\%$.

d) $\ln 0.85 = -0.1625$. The probability that $S_T < 0.85$ is the same as the probability that $\ln S_T < -0.1625$. It is

$$N\left(\frac{-0.1625 + 0.2249}{0.06}\right) = N(1.0404)$$

This is 85.09%. The probability that the exchange rate is between 0.80 and 0.85 is therefore $85.09 - 51.20 = 33.89\%$.

e) $\ln 0.90 = -0.1054$. The probability that $S_T < 0.90$ is the same as the probability that $\ln S_T < -0.1054$. It is

$$N\left(\frac{-0.1054 + 0.2249}{0.06}\right) = N(1.9931)$$

This is 97.69%. The probability that the exchange rate is between 0.85 and 0.90 is therefore $97.69 - 85.09 = 12.60\%$.

f) The probability that the exchange rate is greater than 0.90 is $100 - 97.69 = 2.31\%$.

The volatility smile encountered for foreign exchange options is shown in Figure 19.1 of the text and implies the probability distribution in Figure 19.2. Figure 19.2 suggests that we would expect the probabilities in (a), (c), (d), and (f) to be too low and the probabilities in (b) and (e) to be too high.

Problem 19.16.

The price of a stock is $40. A six-month European call option on the stock with a strike price of $30 has an implied volatility of 35%. A six month European call option on the stock with a strike price of $50 has an implied volatility of 28%. The six-month risk-free rate is 5% and no dividends are expected. Explain why the two implied volatilities are different. Use DerivaGem to calculate the prices of the two options. Use put–call parity to calculate the prices of six-month European put options with strike prices of $30 and $50. Use DerivaGem to calculate the implied volatilities of these two put options.

The difference between the two implied volatilities is consistent with Figure 19.3 in the text. For equities the volatility smile is downward sloping. A high strike price option has a lower implied volatility than a low strike price option. The reason is that traders consider that the probability of a large downward movement in the stock price is higher than that predicted by the lognormal probability distribution. The implied distribution assumed by traders is shown in Figure 19.4. To use DerivaGem to calculate the price of the first option, proceed as follows. Select Equity as the Underlying Type in the first worksheet. Select Black-Scholes European as the Option Type. Input the stock price as 40, volatility as 35%, risk-free rate as 5%, time to exercise as 0.5 year, and exercise price as 30. Leave the dividend table blank because we are assuming no dividends. Select the button corresponding to call. Do not select the implied volatility button. Hit the *Enter* key and click on calculate. DerivaGem will show the price of the option as 11.155. Change the volatility to 28% and the strike price to 50. Hit the *Enter* key and click on calculate. DerivaGem will show the price of the option as 0.725.
Put–call parity is

$$c + Ke^{-rT} = p + S_0$$

so that

$$p = c + Ke^{-rT} - S_0$$

For the first option, $c = 11.155$, $S_0 = 40$, $r = 0.054$, $K = 30$, and $T = 0.5$ so that

$$p = 11.155 + 30e^{-0.05 \times 0.5} - 40 = 0.414$$

For the second option, $c = 0.725$, $S_0 = 40$, $r = 0.06$, $K = 50$, and $T = 0.5$ so that

$$p = 0.725 + 50e^{-0.05 \times 0.5} - 40 = 9.490$$

To use DerivaGem to calculate the implied volatility of the first put option, input the stock price as 40, the risk-free rate as 5%, time to exercise as 0.5 year, and the exercise price as 30. Input the price as 0.414 in the second half of the Option Data table. Select the buttons for a put option and implied volatility. Hit the *Enter* key and click on calculate. DerivaGem will show the implied volatility as 34.99%.
Similarly, to use DerivaGem to calculate the implied volatility of the first put option, input the stock price as 40, the risk-free rate as 5%, time to exercise as 0.5 year, and the exercise price as 50. Input the price as 9.490 in the second half of the Option Data table. Select the buttons for a put option and implied volatility. Hit the *Enter* key and click on calculate. DerivaGem will show

134

the implied volatility as 27.99%.

These results are what we would expect. DerivaGem gives the implied volatility of a put with strike price 30 to be almost exactly the same as the implied volatility of a call with a strike price of 30. Similarly, it gives the implied volatility of a put with strike price 50 to be almost exactly the same as the implied volatility of a call with a strike price of 50.

Problem 19.17.

"The Black–Scholes–Merton model is used by traders as an interpolation tool." Discuss this view.

When plain vanilla call and put options are being priced, traders do use the Black–Scholes–Merton model as an interpolation tool. They calculate implied volatilities for the options whose prices they can observe in the market. By interpolating between strike prices and between times to maturity, they estimate implied volatilities for other options. These implied volatilities are then substituted into Black-Scholes-Merton to calculate prices for these options.

Problem 19.18

Using Table 19.2 calculate the implied volatility a trader would use for an 8-month option with a strike price of 1.04.

The answer is 13.45%. We get the same answer by (a) interpolating between strike prices of 1.00 and 1.05 and then between maturities six months and one year and (b) interpolating between maturities of six months and one year and then between strike prices of 1.00 and 1.05.

CHAPTER 20
Value at Risk and Expected Shortfall

Value at risk (VaR) and expected shortfall (ES) are important risk measures. VaR is the loss on a portfolio that, with a certain confidence level, will not be exceeded. Suppose that the 10-day, 99% VaR is $5.6 million for a bank. This means that the probability of the bank's losses over the next 10 days being greater than $5.6 million is 1%. Bank regulators have traditionally based the capital they require for market risk on a calculation of the 10-day, 99% VaR. ES is the expected loss if the loss is greater than the VaR level. In our example it would be the average of the losses in situations where the loss is greater than $5.6 million.

There are two ways of calculating VaR or ES. The first is historical simulation. The second is the "model building" or "variance-covariance" approach. Historical simulation involves using the history of how market variables have behaved during the last N days to estimate a one-day VaR or ES. It generates N scenarios. The first scenario assumes that the percentage change in all variables between today and tomorrow is the same as that between Day 0 and Day 1 of the historical data; the second scenario assumes that the percentage change in all variables between today and tomorrow is the same as that between Day 1 and Day 2 of the historical data; and so on. The scenarios are used to create a probability distribution for the change in the value of the current portfolio between today and tomorrow. This in turn allows the one-day VaR or ES to be determined. The 10-day VaR (ES) is calculated as the one-day VaR (ES) multiplied by $\sqrt{10}$.

The model building approach uses a model for the daily changes in the values of market variables. Like the historical simulation approach its initial focus is on the one-day VaR or ES. The most common assumption is that the percentage changes in the values of market variables have a multivariate normal distribution. If the change in the value of the portfolio is linearly related to the changes in the values of the variables, the one-day change in the value of the portfolio is normally distributed. The mean change is usually assumed to be zero. The standard deviation of the change can be calculated from the standard deviations of, and correlations between, the market variables. This enables the one-day VaR and one-day ES to be calculated. As in the case of the historical simulation approach, the 10-day VaR (ES) is assumed to be $\sqrt{10}$ times the one-day VaR (ES).

Options create problems for the model building approach. This is because the change in the value of an option is not linearly related to the change in the value of the underlying variables. One approach is to use the delta of the option to define an approximately linear relationship. However, this can lead to serious inaccuracies. Another approach, not easy to implement, is to use delta and gamma and assume a quadratic relationship between the change in the value of the option and changes in the values of the underlying market variables.

The model building approach requires estimates of volatilities and correlations for the market variables. The volatility is the daily volatility and is defined as the standard deviation of percentage daily changes. A popular estimation approach is the exponentially weighted moving average (EWMA) method. This applies weights to observations that decrease exponentially as we move back through time. The nice thing about the EWMA approach is that relatively little data needs to be kept. For example to update a volatility estimate all we need is the most recent change in the market variable (see equation 20.11). Similarly, to update an estimate of the correlation between two variables all we need are the most recent changes in the variables (see equation 20.13) The updating is actually carried out in terms of variances and covariances. The variance is the square of the volatility. The covariance is the correlation multiplied by the product of the volatilities of the two variables.

Answers to Practice Questions

Problem 20.8.
A company uses an EWMA model for forecasting volatility. It decides to change the parameter λ from 0.95 to 0.85. Explain the likely impact on the forecasts.

Reducing λ from 0.95 to 0.85 means that more weight is put on recent observations of u_i^2 and less weight is given to older observations. Volatilities calculated with $\lambda = 0.85$ will react more quickly to new information and will "bounce around" much more than volatilities calculated with $\lambda = 0.95$.

Problem 20.9.
Explain the difference between value at risk and expected shortfall.

Value at risk is the loss that is expected to be exceeded $(100 - X)\%$ of the time in N days for specified parameter values, X and N. Expected shortfall is the expected loss conditional that the loss is greater than the Value at Risk.

Problem 20.10.
Consider a position consisting of a $100,000 investment in asset A and a $100,000 investment in asset B. Assume that the daily volatilities of both assets are 1% and that the coefficient of correlation between their returns is 0.3. What is the 5-day 99% value at risk and expected shortfall for the portfolio?

The standard deviation of the daily change in the investment in each asset is $1,000. The variance of the portfolio's daily change is
$$1,000^2 + 1,000^2 + 2 \times 0.3 \times 1,000 \times 1,000 = 2,600,000$$
The standard deviation of the portfolio's daily change is the square root of this or $1,612.45. The standard deviation of the 5-day change is
$$1,612.45 \times \sqrt{5} = \$3,605.55$$
From the tables of $N(x)$ we see that $N(-2.326)=0.01$. This means that 1% of a normal distribution lies more than 2.326 standard deviations below the mean. The 5-day 99 percent value at risk is therefore 2.326×3,605.55 = $8,388.

The 5-day 99% ES is from equation (20.1)

$$3605.55\frac{e^{-2.326^2/2}}{\sqrt{2\pi}\times 0.01} = \$9,610$$

Problem 20.11.
The volatility of a certain market variable is 30% per annum. Calculate a 99% confidence interval for the size of the percentage daily change in the variable.

The volatility per day is $30/\sqrt{252} = 1.89\%$. There is a 99% chance that a normally distributed variable will be within 2.57 standard deviations. We are therefore 99% confident that the daily change will be less than $2.57 \times 1.89 = 4.86\%$.

Problem 20.12.
Explain how a forward contract to sell a foreign currency is mapped into a portfolio of zero-coupon bonds with standard maturities for the purposes of a VaR calculation.

The contract can be regarded as a short position in a foreign zero coupon bond combined with a long position in a domestic zero coupon bond. Each bond can be mapped into two zero coupon bonds with standard maturities. The foreign zero coupon bond values are expressed in the domestic currency. The relevant volatilities and correlations are therefore (a) the volatilities of two domestic zero coupon bonds, (b) the volatilities of two foreign zero coupon bonds when their values are measured in the domestic currency, and (c) correlations between the returns on the four bonds, all measured in the domestic currency.

Problem 20.13.
Explain why the linear model can provide only approximate estimates of VaR for a portfolio containing options.

The change in the value of an option is not linearly related to the percentage change in the value of the underlying variable. The linear model assumes that the change in the value of a portfolio is linearly related to percentage changes in the underlying variables. It is therefore only an approximation for a portfolio containing options.

Problem 20.14.
Some time ago a company entered into a forward contract to buy £1 million for $1.5 million. The contract now has six months to maturity. The daily volatility of a six-month zero-coupon sterling bond (when its price is translated to dollars) is 0.06% and the daily volatility of a six-month zero-coupon dollar bond is 0.05%. The correlation between returns from the two bonds is 0.8. The current exchange rate is 1.53. Calculate the standard deviation of the change in the dollar value of the forward contract in one day. What is the 10-day 99% VaR? Assume that the six-month interest rate in both sterling and dollars is 5% per annum with continuous compounding.

The contract is a long position in a sterling bond combined with a short position in a dollar bond. The value of the sterling bond is $1.53e^{-0.05\times 0.5}$ or $1.492 million. The value of the dollar bond is $1.5e^{-0.05\times 0.5}$ or $1.463 million. The variance of the change in the value of the contract in one day

is
$$1.492^2 \times 0.0006^2 + 1.463^2 \times 0.0005^2 - 2 \times 0.8 \times 1.492 \times 0.0006 \times 1.463 \times 0.0005$$
$$= 0.000000288$$

The standard deviation is therefore $0.000537 million. The 10-day 99% VaR is $0.000537 \times \sqrt{10} \times 2.33 = \$0.00396$ million.

Problem 20.15.
The most recent estimate of the daily volatility of the U.S. dollar–sterling exchange rate is 0.6%, and the exchange rate at 4 p.m. yesterday was 1.5000. The parameter λ in the EWMA model is 0.9. Suppose that the exchange rate at 4 p.m. today proves to be 1.4950. How would the estimate of the daily volatility be updated?

The daily return is $-0.005 / 1.5000 = -0.003333$. The current daily variance estimate is $0.006^2 = 0.000036$. The new daily variance estimate is
$$0.9 \times 0.000036 + 0.1 \times 0.003333^2 = 0.000033511$$
The new volatility is the square root of this. It is 0.00579 or 0.579%.

Problem 20.16.
Suppose that the daily volatilities of asset A and asset B calculated at close of trading yesterday are 1.6% and 2.5%, respectively. The prices of the assets at close of trading yesterday were $20 and $40, and the estimate of the coefficient of correlation between the returns on the two assets made at close of trading yesterday was 0.25. The parameter λ used in the EWMA model is 0.95.
(a) Calculate the current estimate of the covariance between the assets.
(b) On the assumption that the prices of the assets at close of trading today are $20.5 and $40.5, update the correlation estimate.

a) The volatilities and correlation imply that the current estimate of the covariance is $0.25 \times 0.016 \times 0.025 = 0.0001$.
b) If the prices of the assets at close of trading today are $20.5 and $40.5, the returns are $0.5 / 20 = 0.025$ and $0.5 / 40 = 0.0125$. The new covariance estimate is
$$0.95 \times 0.0001 + 0.05 \times 0.025 \times 0.0125 = 0.0001106$$
The new variance estimate for asset A is
$$0.95 \times 0.016^2 + 0.05 \times 0.025^2 = 0.00027445$$
so that the new volatility is 0.0166. The new variance estimate for asset B is
$$0.95 \times 0.025^2 + 0.05 \times 0.0125^2 = 0.000601562$$
so that the new volatility is 0.0245. The new correlation estimate is
$$\frac{0.0001106}{0.0166 \times 0.0245} = 0.272$$

Problem 20.17.
Suppose that the daily volatility of the FT-SE 100 stock index (measured in pounds sterling) is 1.8% and the daily volatility of the dollar/sterling exchange rate is 0.9%. Suppose further that the correlation between the FT-SE 100 and the dollar/sterling exchange rate is 0.4. What is the

volatility of the FT-SE 100 when it is translated to U.S. dollars? Assume that the dollar/sterling exchange rate is expressed as the number of U.S. dollars per pound sterling. (Hint: When Z = XY , the percentage daily change in Z is approximately equal to the percentage daily change in X plus the percentage daily change in Y .)

The FT-SE expressed in dollars is XY where X is the FT-SE expressed in sterling and Y is the exchange rate (value of one pound in dollars). Define x_i as the proportional change in X on day i and y_i as the proportional change in Y on day i. The proportional change in XY is approximately $x_i + y_i$. The standard deviation of x_i is 0.018 and the standard deviation of y_i is 0.009. The correlation between the two is 0.4. The variance of $x_i + y_i$ is therefore

$$0.018^2 + 0.009^2 + 2 \times 0.018 \times 0.009 \times 0.4 = 0.0005346$$

so that the volatility of $x_i + y_i$ is 0.0231 or 2.31%. This is the volatility of the FT-SE expressed in dollars. Note that it is greater than the volatility of the FT-SE expressed in sterling. This is the impact of the positive correlation. When the FT-SE increases, the value of sterling measured in dollars also tends to increase. This creates an even bigger increase in the value of FT-SE measured in dollars. A similar result holds for a decrease in the FT-SE.

Problem 20.18.
Suppose that in Problem 20.17 the correlation between the S&P 500 Index (measured in dollars) and the FT-SE 100 Index (measured in sterling) is 0.7, the correlation between the S&P 500 index (measured in dollars) and the dollar-sterling exchange rate is 0.3, and the daily volatility of the S&P 500 Index is 1.6%. What is the correlation between the S&P 500 Index (measured in dollars) and the FT-SE 100 Index when it is translated to dollars? (Hint: For three variables X , Y , and Z , the covariance between X +Y and Z equals the covariance between X and Z plus the covariance between Y and Z .)

Continuing with the notation in Problem 20.17, define z_i as the proportional change in the value of the S&P 500 on day i. The covariance between x_i and z_i is $0.7 \times 0.018 \times 0.016 = 0.0002016$. The covariance between y_i and z_i is $0.3 \times 0.009 \times 0.016 = 0.0000432$. The covariance between $x_i + y_i$ and z_i equals the covariance between x_i and z_i plus the covariance between y_i and z_i. It is

$$0.0002016 + 0.0000432 = 0.0002448$$

The correlation between $x_i + y_i$ and z_i is

$$\frac{0.0002448}{0.016 \times 0.0231} = 0.662$$

Problem 20.19.
The one-day 99% VaR is calculated for the four-index example in Section 20.2 as $253,385. Look at the underlying spreadsheets on the author's web site and calculate a) the one-day 95% VaR, b) the one-day 95% ES, c) the one-day 97% VaR, and d) the one-day 97% ES

The 95% one-day VaR is the 25th worst loss. This is $156,511. (b) The 95% one-day ES is the average of the 25 highest losses. It is $207,198. (c) The 97% one-day VaR is the 15th worst loss. This is $172,224. (d) The 97% one-day ES is the average of the 15 highest losses. It is $236,297.

Problem 20.20.
Use the spreadsheets on the author's web site to calculate the one-day 99% VaR and ES, using the basic methodology in Section 20.2 if the four-index portfolio considered in Section 20.2 is equally divided between the four indices.

In worksheet 2 (Scenarios), the portfolio investments are changed to 2,500 in cells L2:O2. The losses are then sorted from the largest to the smallest. The fifth worst loss is $238,526. This is the one-day 99% VaR. The average of the five worst losses is $346,003. This is the one-day 99% ES.

Problem 20.21.
At the end of Section 20.6, VaR and ES for the four-index example were calculated using the model-building approach. How do the VaR and ES estimates change if the investment is $2.5 million in each index? Carry out calculations when a) volatilities and correlations are estimated using the equally weighted model and b) when they are estimated using the EWMA model with $\lambda = 0.94$. Use the spreadsheets on the author's web site.

The alphas should be changed to 2,500. This changes the one-day 99% VaR to $226,836 and the one-day ES to $259,878 when volatilities and correlations are estimated using the equally weighted model. It changes the one-day 99% VaR to $487,737 and the one-day 99% ES to $558,783 when EWMA with $\lambda = 0.94$ is used.

Problem 20.22.
What is the effect of changing λ from 0.94 to 0.97 in the EWMA calculations in the four-index example at the end of Section 20.6? Use the spreadsheets on the author's web site.

The parameter λ is in cell N3 of the EWMA worksheet. Changing it to 0.97 changes the one-day 99% VaR from $471,025 to $389,290. This is because less weight is given to recent observations. ES is changed from $539,637 to $445,996.

CHAPTER 21
Interest Rate Options

The chapter describes the most common interest rate options and the standard market models that are used to price them. The exchange-traded interest rate options considered are options on Eurodollar futures and options on Treasury bond futures. They can be valued using the approach in Chapter 16. The over-the-counter products considered are European bond options, interest rate caps and floors, and European swap options.

European options on bonds are traded in the over-the-counter market. Typically an implied yield volatility is quoted. This yield volatility is converted into a price volatility (see equation 21.6) using an approximate duration result and the price volatility is used in a Black-Scholes-Merton type of formula where the bond price at the maturity of the option is assumed to be lognormal.

An interest-rate cap is an instrument that provides insurance against the rate paid on a floating rate loan going above a certain level. The level (known as the cap rate) is analogous to the strike price in a regular option. The rate on the floating rate loan is reset every month, every quarter, every six months, or every year. An interest rate cap therefore consists of a series of call options on future interest rates, one corresponding to each time the floating rate is reset. The individual options are referred to as caplets. Each caplet is valued using a Black-Scholes-Merton type of formula where the future interest rate is assumed to be lognormally distributed. (See equation 21.8.)

For any call option there is a corresponding put option. Interest rate caps are no exception. Just as an interest rate cap is a series of call options on interest rates, an interest rate floor is a series of put options on interest rates. As shown in Business Snapshot 21.1 there is a relationship between the values of an interest rate floor, an interest rate cap, and a swap. This is similar to the put-call parity relationship for regular call and put options.

A European swap option (often called a European swaption) is an option to enter into a swap at a particular future time.   In the swap, a fixed rate is exchanged for LIBOR. The fixed rate is analogous to the strike price in a regular option and is specified at the time the swaption is entered into. A swaption where the holder has the right to pay fixed and receive floating can be viewed as a call option on the swap rate (or as a put option on a par yield bond). A swaption where the holder has the right to receive fixed and pay floating can be viewed as a put option on the swap rate (or a call option on a par yield bond). A European swaption is valued by assuming that the swap rate at the maturity of the swap option is lognormally distributed (see equations 21.10 and 21.11).

Software

The Bond_Options and Cap_and_Swaptions worksheets in DG400f.xls allow interest rate options to be valued using the models introduced in this chapter.

Answers to Practice Questions

Problem 21.8.

A bank uses Black's model to price European bond options. Suppose that an implied price volatility for a 5-year option on a bond maturing in 10 years is used to price a 9-year option on the bond. Would you expect the resultant price to be too high or too low? Explain your answer.

The volatility of the forward price of a bond that will have one year remaining at the maturity of the forward contract is less than the volatility of a bond that will have five years remaining at the maturity of the forward contract. The volatility used to price a nine-year option on a ten-year bond should therefore be less than that used to price a five-year option on a ten-year bond. Using the volatility backed out from the five-year option to price the nine-year option is therefore likely to produce a price that is too high.

Problem 21.9.

Consider a four-year European call option on a bond that will mature in five years. The five-year bond price is $105, the price of a four-year bond with the same coupon as the five-year bond is $102, the strike price of the option is $100, the four-year risk-free interest rate is 10% per annum (continuously compounded), and the volatility of the forward price of the bond underlying the option is 2% per annum. What is the present value of the principal in the four-year bond? What is the present value of the coupons in the four-year bond? What is the forward price of the bond underlying the option? What is the value of the option?

The present value of the principal in the four year bond is $100e^{-4\times0.1} = 67.032$. The present value of the coupons is, therefore, $102 - 67.032 = 34.968$. The coupons on the four-year bond are the income on the five-year bond during the life of the option. This means that the forward price of the bond underlying the option is

$$(105 - 34.968)e^{0.1\times4} = 104.475$$

The parameters in Black's model are therefore $F_0 = 104.475$, $K = 100$, $r = 0.1$, $T = 4$, and $\sigma = 0.02$.

$$d_1 = \frac{\ln 1.04475 + 0.5\times0.02^2\times4}{0.02\sqrt{4}} = 1.1144$$

$$d_2 = d_1 - 0.02\sqrt{4} = 1.0744$$

The price of the European call is

$$e^{-0.1\times4}[104.475N(1.1144) - 100N(1.0744)] = 3.19$$

or $3.19.

Problem 21.10.

If the yield volatility for a five-year put option on a bond maturing in 10 years time is specified as 22%, how should the option be valued? Assume that, based on today's interest rates the modified duration of the bond at the maturity of the option will be 4.2 years and the forward yield on the bond is 7%.

The relationship between the yield volatility and the price volatility is given by equation (21.6).

143

In this case, the price volatility is
$$0.07 \times 4.2 \times 0.22 = 6.47\%$$
This is the volatility substituted into equation (21.2).

Problem 21.11.

A corporation knows that in three months it will have $5 million to invest for 90 days at LIBOR minus 50 basis points and wishes to ensure that the rate obtained will be at least 6.5%. What position in exchange-traded interest-rate options should the corporation take?

The rate received will be less than 6.5% when LIBOR is less than 7%. The corporation requires a three-month call option on a Eurodollar futures option with a strike price of 93. If three-month LIBOR is greater than 7% at the option maturity, the Eurodollar futures quote at option maturity will be less than 93 and there will be no payoff from the option. If the three-month LIBOR is less than 7%, one Eurodollar futures options provide a payoff of $25 per 0.01%. Each 0.01% of interest costs the corporation $500 ($= 5,000,000 \times 0.0001$). A total of $500 / 25 = 20$ contracts are therefore required.

Problem 21.12.

Explain carefully how you would use (a) spot volatilities and (b) flat volatilities to value a five-year cap.

When spot volatilities are used to value a cap, a different volatility is used to value each caplet. When flat volatilities are used, the same volatility is used to value each caplet within a given cap. Spot volatilities are a function of the maturity of the caplet. Flat volatilities are a function of the maturity of the cap.

Problem 21.13.

What other instrument is the same as a five-year zero-cost collar in which the strike price of the cap equals the strike price of the floor? What does the common strike price equal?

A 5-year zero-cost collar where the strike price of the cap equals the strike price of the floor is the same as an interest rate swap agreement to receive floating and pay a fixed rate equal to the strike price. The common strike price is the swap rate. Note that the swap is actually a forward swap that excludes the first exchange of payments (see Business Snapshot 21.1).

Problem 21.14.

Suppose that all risk-free (OIS) zero rates are 6.5% (continuously compounded). The price of a 5-year semiannual cap with a principal of $100 and a cap rate of 8% (semiannually compounded) is $3. Use DerivaGem to determine:
(a) The 5-year implied flat volatility for caps and floors
(b) The floor rate in a zero-cost 5-year collar when the cap rate is 8%.
Assume that all six-month LIBOR forward rates are 6.7% with semiannual compounding.

Choose the Caps and Swap Options worksheet of DerivaGem and choose Cap/Floor as the Underlying Type. Enter the zero rates as 6.5%. (It is only necessary to enter this for one maturity as the rate for all maturities will then automatically be assumed to be 6.5%). The LIBOR forward rates are input as 6.7%. (Again this only need to be done for one maturity.) Enter Semiannual for the Settlement Frequency, 100 for the Principal, 0 for the Start (Years), 5 for the End (Years), 8% for the Cap/Floor Rate, and $3 for the Price. Check the Cap button. Check the Imply Volatility box and hit *Calculate*. The implied volatility is 31.51%. Then uncheck Implied Volatility, select Floor, check Imply Breakeven Rate. The floor rate that is calculated is 5.9%. This is the floor rate for which the floor is worth $3. A collar when the floor rate is 5.9% and the cap rate is 8% has zero cost.

Problem 21.15.

Show that $V_1 + f = V_2$ where V_1 is the value of a swaption to pay a fixed rate of R_K and receive LIBOR between times T_1 and T_2, f is the value of a forward swap to receive a fixed rate of R_K and pay LIBOR between times T_1 and T_2, and V_2 is the value of a swaption to receive a fixed rate of R_K between times T_1 and T_2. Deduce that $V_1 = V_2$ when R_K equals the current forward swap rate.

We prove this result by considering two portfolios. The first consists of the swap option to receive R_K; the second consists of the swap option to pay R_K and the forward swap. Suppose that the actual swap rate at the maturity of the options is greater than R_K. The swap option to pay R_K will be exercised and the swap option to receive R_K will not be exercised. Both portfolios are then worth zero since the swap option to pay R_K is neutralized by the forward swap. Suppose next that the actual swap rate at the maturity of the options is less than R_K. The swap option to receive R_K is exercised and the swap option to pay R_K is not exercised. Both portfolios are then equivalent to a swap where R_K is received and floating is paid. In all states of the world the two portfolios are worth the same at time T_1. They must therefore be worth the same today. This proves the result. When R_K equals the current forward swap rate $f = 0$ and $V_1 = V_2$. A swap option to pay fixed is therefore worth the same as a similar swap option to receive fixed when the fixed rate in the swap option is the forward swap rate.

Problem 21.16.

Explain why there is an arbitrage opportunity if the implied Black (flat) volatility for a cap is different from that for a floor.

The put–call parity relationship in Business Snapshot 21.1 is
$$cap + swap = floor$$
must hold for market prices. It also holds for Black's model. An argument similar to that in the appendix to Chapter 19 shows that the implied volatility of the cap must equal the implied volatility of the call. If this is not the case there is an arbitrage opportunity. (NB: The final sentence of this question in the text should be deleted as there is no Table 21.1.)

Problem 21.17.

Suppose that zero rates and LIBOR forward rates are as in Problem 21.14. Use DerivaGem to determine the value of an option to pay a fixed rate of 6% and receive LIBOR on a five-year *swap starting in one year. Assume that the principal is $100 million, payments are exchanged semiannually, and the swap rate volatility is 21%.*

Choose the Caps and Swap Options worksheet of DerivaGem and choose Swap Option as the Underlying Type. Enter 100 as the Principal, 1 as the Start (Years), 6 as the End (Years), 6% as the Swap Rate, and Semiannual as the Settlement Frequency. Enter 21% as the Volatility and check the Pay Fixed button. Do not check the Imply Breakeven Rate or Imply Volatility boxes. The value of the swap option is 3.75.

CHAPTER 22
Exotic Options and Other Nonstandard Products

Derivatives traders have been very imaginative in designing new derivative instruments. This chapter gives you a flavor for the nonstandard products that exist. It introduces exotic options, mortgage-backed securities, and non-standard swaps. Some of the instruments covered are designed to meet the hedging needs of corporate treasurers or fund managers; some are designed for tax, accounting, legal or regulatory reasons; some are simply interesting alternatives to the "plain vanilla" products.

The exotic options discussed include Bermudan options, forward start options, compound options, chooser options, barrier options, binary options, lookback options, shout options, and Asian options.

Agency mortgage-backed securities (MBSs) are important instruments in the United States. They are created when a financial institution securitizes part of its residential mortgage portfolio. The mortgages are put in a pool and investors acquire a stake in the pool by buying units. The mortgages are guaranteed against defaults by a government agency, but there is prepayment risk. As rates decline there is a tendency for mortgage holders to prepay. The prepayments are passed on to the MBS holders who then have to reinvest the funds at a lower rate of interest than they were earning before. Often mortgage-backed securities are designed so that different investors bear different amounts of prepayment risk.

The final part of the chapter discusses non-standard swaps. These are variations on the swaps discussed in Chapter 7. Among the different types of swaps discussed are those where the principal changes through time, where the floating interest rate is not LIBOR, where interest is compounded forward rather than being paid out, LIBOR-in-arrears swaps, CMS swaps, differential swaps, equity swaps, accrual swaps, cancelable swaps, commodity swaps, and volatility swaps.

Software

The Equity_FX_Indx_Fut_Opts_Calc worksheet in DG400f.xls allow some of the exotic options introduced in this chapter to be valued. See the Option Type drop down menu.

Answers to Practice Questions

Problem 22.8.
Describe the payoff from a portfolio consisting of a floating lookback call and a floating lookback put with the same maturity.

A floating lookback call provides a payoff of $S_T - S_{min}$. A floating lookback put provides a payoff of $S_{max} - S_T$. A combination of the lookback call and the lookback put therefore provides a payoff of $S_{max} - S_{min}$.

Problem 22.9.

Consider a chooser option where the holder has the right to choose between a European call and a European put at any time during a two-year period. The maturity dates and strike prices for the calls and puts are the same regardless of when the choice is made. Is it ever optimal to make the choice before the end of the two-year period? Explain your answer.

No, it is never optimal to choose early. The resulting cash flows are the same regardless of when the choice is made. There is no point in the holder making a commitment earlier than necessary. This argument also applies when the holder chooses between two American options providing the options cannot be exercised before the two-year point. If the early exercise period starts as soon as the choice is made, the argument does not hold. For example, if the stock price fell to almost nothing in the first six months, the holder would choose a put option at this time and exercise it immediately.

Problem 22.10.

Suppose that c_1 and p_1 are the prices of a European average price call and a European average price put with strike price K and maturity T, c_2 and p_2 are the prices of a European average strike call and European average strike put with maturity T, and c_3 and p_3 are the prices of a regular European call and a regular European put with strike price K and maturity T. Show that

$$c_1 + c_2 - c_3 = p_1 + p_2 - p_3$$

The payoffs are as follows:

c_1 : $\max(S_{ave} - K, 0)$

c_2 : $\max(S_T - S_{ave}, 0)$

c_3 : $\max(S_T - K, 0)$

p_1 : $\max(K - S_{ave}, 0)$

p_2 : $\max(S_{ave} - S_T, 0)$

p_3 : $\max(K - S_T, 0)$

The payoff from $c_1 - p_1$ is always $S_{ave} - K$; The payoff from $c_2 - p_2$ is always $S_T - S_{ave}$; The payoff from $c_3 - p_3$ is always $S_T - K$; It follows that

$$c_1 - p_1 + c_2 - p_2 = c_3 - p_3$$

or

$$c_1 + c_2 - c_3 = p_1 + p_2 - p_3$$

Problem 22.11.

The text derives a decomposition of a particular type of chooser option into a call maturing at time T_2 and a put maturing at time T_1. By using put–call parity to obtain an expression for c *instead of* p, *derive an alternative decomposition into a call maturing at time* T_1 *and a put maturing at time* T_2.

Substituting for c, put-call parity gives

$$\max(c, p) = \max\left[p, p + S_1 e^{-q(T_2-T_1)} - Ke^{-r(T_2-T_1)}\right]$$

$$= p + \max\left[0, S_1 e^{-q(T_2-T_1)} - Ke^{-r(T_2-T_1)}\right]$$

$$= p + e^{-q(T_2-T_1)}\max\left[0, S_1 - Ke^{-(r-q)(T_2-T_1)}\right]$$

This shows that the chooser option can be decomposed into a) a put option with strike price K and maturity T_2 and b) $e^{-q(T_2-T_1)}$ call options with strike price $Ke^{-(r-q)(T_2-T_1)}$ and maturity T_1.

Problem 22.12.
Explain why a down-and-out put is worth zero when the barrier is greater than the strike price.

The option is in the money only when the asset price is less than the strike price. However, in these circumstances the barrier has been hit and the option has ceased to exist.

Problem 22.13.
Prove that an at-the-money forward start option on a non-dividend-paying stock that will start in three years and mature in five years is worth the same as a two-year at-the-money option starting today.

Suppose that c is the value of a two-year option starting today. Define S_0 as the stock price today and S_T as its value in three years. The Black-Scholes-Merton formula in Chapter 13 shows that the value of an at-the-money option is proportional to the stock price when there are no dividends. It follows that the value of the forward start option in three years is cS_T / S_0. We can now use risk-neutral valuation. The expected value of the option in three years in a risk-neutral world is $cS_0 e^{rT} / S_0 = ce^{rT}$. Discounting this to today at the risk-free rate gives c, proving the required result.

Problem 22.14.
Suppose that the strike price of an American call option on a non-dividend-paying stock grows at rate g. *Show that if* g *is less than the risk-free rate,* r, *it is never optimal to exercise the call early.*

The argument is similar to that given in Chapter 10 for a regular option on a non-dividend-paying stock. Consider a portfolio consisting of the option and cash equal to the present value of the terminal strike price. The initial cash position is

$$Ke^{gT-rT}$$

By time τ $(0 \le \tau \le T)$, the cash grows to

$$Ke^{gT-rT}e^{r\tau} = Ke^{g\tau}e^{-(r-g)(T-\tau)}$$

Since $r > g$, this is less than $Ke^{g\tau}$ and therefore is less than the amount required to exercise the option. It follows that, if the option is exercised early, the terminal value of the portfolio is less than S_T. At time T the cash balance is Ke^{gT}. This is exactly what is required to exercise the option. If the early exercise decision is delayed until time T, the terminal value of the portfolio is therefore $\max(S_T, Ke^{gT})$. This is at least as great as S_T. It follows that early exercise cannot be optimal.

Problem 22.15.

Answer the following questions about compound options:
(a) What put–call parity relationship exists between the price of a European call on a call and a European put on a call?
(b) What put–call parity relationship exists between the price of a European call on a put and a European put on a put?

a) The put–call relationship is
$$cc + K_1 e^{-rT_1} = pc + c$$
where cc is the price of the call on the call, pc is the price of the put on the call, c is the price today of the call into which the options can be exercised at time T_1, and K_1 is the exercise price for cc and pc. The proof is similar to that for the usual put–call parity relationship in Chapter 10. Both sides of the equation represent the values of portfolios that will be worth $\max(c, K_1)$ at time T_1.

b) The put–call relationship is
$$cp + K_1 e^{-rT_1} = pp + p$$
where cp is the price of the call on the put, pp is the price of the put on the put, p is the price today of the put into which the options can be exercised at time T_1, and K_1 is the exercise price for cp and pp. The proof is similar to that in Chapter 10 for the usual put–call parity relationship. Both sides of the equation represent the values of portfolios that will be worth $\max(p, K_1)$ at time T_1.

Problem 22.16.

Does a floating lookback call become more valuable or less valuable as we increase the frequency with which we observe the asset price in calculating the minimum?

As we increase the frequency we observe a more extreme minimum. This increases the value of a lookback call.

Problem 22.17.

Does a down-and-out call become more valuable or less valuable as we increase the frequency with which we observe the asset price in determining whether the barrier has been crossed? What is the answer to the same question for a down-and-in call?

As we increase the frequency with which the asset price is observed, the asset price becomes more likely to hit the barrier and the value of a down-and-out call decreases. For a similar reason the value of a down-and-in call increases.

Problem 22.18.
Explain why a regular European call option is the sum of a down-and-out European call and a down-and-in European call.

If the barrier is reached the down-and-out option is worth nothing while the down-and-in option has the same value as a regular option. If the barrier is not reached the down-and-in option is worth nothing while the down-and-out option has the same value as a regular option. This is why a down-and-out call option plus a down-and-in call option is worth the same as a regular option.

Problem 22.19.
What is the value of a derivative that pays off $100 in six months if the S&P 500 index is greater than 1,000 and zero otherwise. Assume that the current level of the index is 960, the risk-free rate is 8% per annum, the dividend yield on the index is 3% per annum, and the volatility of the index is 20%.

This is a cash-or-nothing call. The value is $100N(d_2)e^{-0.08\times0.5}$ where

$$d_2 = \frac{\ln(960/1000)+(0.08-0.03-0.2^2/2)\times0.5}{0.2\times\sqrt{0.5}} = -0.1826$$

Because $N(d_2)=0.4276$ the value of the derivative is $41.08.

Problem 22.20.
Estimate the interest rate paid by P&G on the 5/30 swap in Business Snapshot 22.4 if a) the CP rate is 6.5% and the Treasury yield curve is flat at 6% and b) the CP rate is 7.5% and the Treasury yield curve is flat at 7%.

When the CP rate is 6.5% and Treasury rates are 6% with semiannual compounding, the CMT% is 6% and an Excel spreadsheet can be used to show that the price of a 30-year bond with a 6.25% coupon is about 103.46. The spread is zero and the rate paid by P&G is 5.75%. When the CP rate is 7.5% and Treasury rates are 7% with semiannual compounding, the CMT% is 7% and the price of a 30-year bond with a 6.25% coupon is about 90.65. The spread is therefore
$$\max[0,(98.5\times7/5.78-90.65)/100]$$
or 28.64%. The rate paid by P&G is 35.39%.

CHAPTER 23
Credit Derivatives

Credit derivatives are contracts where the payoff depends on the creditworthiness of companies or countries. Usually the payoff is triggered by a default on outstanding debt obligations.

The most popular credit derivative is a credit default swap (CDS). This is designed to provide bond holders with insurance against defaults by a particular company or country for a period of time. The company or country is known as the reference entity. A notional principal is specified. The buyer of a CDS makes regular payments to the seller of the CDS. The payments are a certain percentage of the notional principal each year. This percentage is referred to as the CDS spread. (Thus if the CDS spread is 200 basis points the payments are 2% of the notional principal each year.) If there is no default, the buyer of the CDS gets nothing in return for the payments. If there is a default, the buyer obtains a payoff which is equivalent to the gain from being able to sell bonds issued by the reference entity for their face value. The total face value of the bonds that can be sold equals the notional principal. You should study Tables 23.2 to 23.5 carefully to make sure you understand all the details of how CDSs work and how they are valued.

Note that the valuation of a credit default swap really involves nothing more than present value arithmetic. We calculate the present value of the expected payments and the present value of the expected payoffs. The CDS spread quoted for a new deal is the CDS spread per annum that equates the present value of expected payments to the present value of expected payoffs. Note also how the recovery rate is defined. It is estimated as the ratio of the value of a bond just after a default to the face value of the bond. It follows that the payoff from a CDS in the event of a default is $L(1-R)$ where L is the principal and R is the recovery rate.

The valuation of a credit default swap requires estimates of the risk neutral probabilities of default during each year of its life. These are sometimes estimated from bond prices and sometimes implied from the spreads quoted for credit default swaps themselves. (Estimating spreads from actively traded CDSs and using them to price other CDSs is analogous to what traders do when using implied volatilities for valuing options.) Make sure you understand the difference between conditional probabilities of default and unconditional probabilities of default. The hazard rate at time t, $h(t)$, corresponds to a conditional probability of default. It is the rate at which defaults are happening at time t. The expression $h(t)\Delta t$ is the probability of default between times t and $t+\Delta t$ conditional on no earlier default.

Other credit derivatives you should understand are binary credit default swaps, basket credit default swaps, total return swaps, credit default swap forwards, credit default swap options, and collateralized debt obligations. Binary credit default swaps provide a predetermined cash payoff in the event of a default. Basket credit default swaps provide a payoff at the time of the nth default from a set of N companies ($N \geq n$). Total return swaps are agreements to exchange the total return on an asset (or portfolio of assets) for LIBOR plus a spread. A credit default swap forward is an obligation to buy or sell a credit default swap in the future. A credit default swap option is the right to buy or sell a credit default swap in the future. Collateralized debt obligations are arrangements whereby the default risk on a portfolio of bonds is shared between different investors. Typically some investors have very little default risk exposure while others have high exposures.

Software

The CDSs worksheet in DG400f.xls allows CDS spreads to be calculated from hazard rates and vice versa.

Answers to Practice Questions

Problem 23.8.

Suppose that the risk-free zero curve is flat at 7% per annum with continuous compounding and that defaults can occur half way through each year in a new five-year credit default swap. Suppose that the recovery rate is 30% and hazard rate is 3%. Estimate the credit default swap spread? Assume payments are made annually.

The table corresponding to Tables 23.2, giving unconditional default probabilities, is

Time (years)	Probability of surviving to year end	Default Probability during year
1	0.9704	0.0296
2	0.9418	0.0287
3	0.9139	0.0278
4	0.8869	0.0270
5	0.8607	0.0262

The table corresponding to Table 23.3, giving the present value of the expected regular payments (payment rate is s per year), is

Time (yrs)	Probability of survival	Expected Payment	Discount Factor	PV of Expected Payment
1	0.9704	0.9704s	0.9324	0.9048s
2	0.9418	0.9418s	0.8694	0.8187s
3	0.9139	0.9139s	0.8106	0.7408s
4	0.8869	0.8869s	0.7558	0.6703s
5	0.8607	0.8607s	0.7047	0.6065s
Total				3.7412s

The table corresponding to Table 23.4, giving the present value of the expected payoffs (notional principal =$1), is

Time (yrs)	Probability of default	Recovery Rate	Expected Payoff	Discount Factor	PV of Expected Payment
0.5	0.0296	0.3	0.0207	0.9656	0.0200
1.5	0.0287	0.3	0.0201	0.9003	0.0181
2.5	0.0278	0.3	0.0195	0.8395	0.0164
3.5	0.0270	0.3	0.0189	0.7827	0.0148
4.5	0.0262	0.3	0.0183	0.7298	0.0134
Total					0.0826

The table corresponding to Table 23.5, giving the present value of accrual payments, is

Time (yrs)	Probability of default	Expected Accrual Payment	Discount Factor	PV of Expected Accrual Payment
0.5	0.0296	0.0148s	0.9656	0.0143s
1.5	0.0287	0.0143s	0.9003	0.0129s
2.5	0.0278	0.0139s	0.8395	0.0117s
3.5	0.0270	0.0135s	0.7827	0.0106s
4.5	0.0262	0.0131s	0.7298	0.0096s
Total				0.0590s

The credit default swap spread s is given by:
$$3.7412s + 0.0590s = 0.0826$$

It is 0.0217 or 217 basis points. This can be verified with DerivaGem.

Problem 23.9.
What is the value of the swap in Problem 23.8 per dollar of notional principal to the protection buyer if the credit default swap spread is 150 basis points?

If the credit default swap spread is 150 basis points, the value of the swap to the buyer of protection is:
$$0.0826 - (3.7312 + 0.0590) \times 0.0150 = 0.0256$$
per dollar of notional principal.

Problem 23.10.
What is the credit default swap spread in Problem 23.8 if it is a binary CDS?

If the swap is a binary CDS, the present value of expected payoffs per dollar of notional principal is 0.0826/0.7= 0.1180 so that
$$3.7412s + 0.0590s = 0.1197$$
The spread, s, is 0.0310 or 310 basis points.

Problem 23.11.
How does a five-year n th-to-default credit default swap work. Consider a basket of 100

reference entities where each reference entity has a probability of defaulting in each year of 1%. As the default correlation between the reference entities increases what would you expect to happen to the value of the swap when a) $n = 1$ and b) $n = 25$. Explain your answer.

A five-year n th to default credit default swap works in the same way as a regular credit default swap except that there is a basket of companies. The payoff occurs when the n th default from the companies in the basket occurs. After the n th default has occurred the swap ceases to exist. When $n = 1$ (so that the swap is a "first to default") an increase in the default correlation lowers the value of the swap. When the default correlation is zero there are 100 independent events that can lead to a payoff. As the correlation increases the probability of a payoff decreases. In the limit when the correlation is perfect there is in effect only one company and therefore only one event that can lead to a payoff.

When $n = 25$ (so that the swap is a 25th to default) an increase in the default correlation increases the value of the swap. When the default correlation is zero there is virtually no chance that there will be 25 defaults and the value of the swap is very close to zero. As the correlation increases the probability of multiple defaults increases. In the limit when the correlation is perfect there is in effect only one company and the value of a 25th-to-default credit default swap is the same as the value of a first-to-default swap.

Problem 23.12.
How is the recovery rate of a bond usually defined? What is the formula relating the payoff on a CDS to the notional principal and the recovery rate?

The recovery rate of a bond is usually defined as the value of the bond a few days after a default occurs as a percentage of the bond's face value. The payoff on a CDS is $L(1 - R)$ where L is the notional principal and R is the recovery rate.

Problem 23.13.
Show that the spread for a new plain vanilla CDS should be $1 - R$ times the spread for a similar new binary CDS where R is the recovery rate.

The payoff from a plain vanilla CDS is $1 - R$ times the payoff from a binary CDS with the same principal. The payoff always occurs at the same time on the two instruments. It follows that the regular payments on a new plain vanilla CDS must be $1 - R$ times the payments on a new binary CDS. Otherwise there would be an arbitrage opportunity.

Problem 23.14.
Verify that, if the CDS spread for the example in Tables 23.2 to 23.5 is 100 basis points, the hazard rate is 1.63% per year. How does the hazard rate change when the recovery rate is 20% instead of 40%. Verify that your answer is consistent with the implied hazard rate being approximately proportional to $1 / (1 - R)$ where R is the recovery rate.

The 1.63% hazard rate can be calculated by setting up a worksheet in Excel and using Solver. To verify that 1.63% is correct we note that, with a hazard rate of 1.63%

Time (years)	Probability of surviving to year end	Default Probability during year
1	0.9838	0.0162
2	0.9679	0.0159
3	0.9523	0.0156
4	0.9369	0.0154
5	0.9217	0.0151

The present value of the regular payments becomes $4.1162s$, the present value of the expected payoffs becomes 0.0416, and the present value of the expected accrual payments becomes $0.0347s$. When $s = 0.01$ the present value of the expected payments equals the present value of the expected payoffs.

When the recovery rate is 20% the implied hazard rate(calculated using Solver) is 1.22% per year. Note that $1.22/1.63$ is approximately equal to $(1-0.4)/(1-0.2)$ showing that the implied hazard is approximately proportional to $1/(1-R)$.

In passing we note that if the CDS spread is used to imply an unconditional default probability (assumed to be the same each year) then this implied unconditional default probability is exactly proportional to $1/(1-R)$. When we use the CDS spread to imply a hazard rate (assumed to be the same each year) it is only approximately proportional to $1/(1-R)$.

Problem 23.15.
A company enters into a total return swap where it receives the return on a corporate bond paying a coupon of 5% and pays LIBOR. Explain the difference between this and a regular swap where 5% is exchanged for LIBOR.

In the case of a total return swap a company receives (pays) the increase (decrease) in the value of the bond. In a regular swap this does not happen.

Problem 23.16.
Explain how forward contracts and options on credit default swaps are structured.

When a company enters into a long (short) forward contract it is obligated to buy (sell) the protection given by a specified credit default swap with a specified spread at a specified future time. When a company buys a call (put) option contract it has the option to buy (sell) the protection given by a specified credit default swap with a specified spread at a specified future time. Both contracts are normally structured so that they cease to exist if a default occurs during the life of the contract.

Problem 23.17.
"The position of a buyer of a credit default swap is similar to the position of someone who is long a risk-free bond and short a corporate bond." Explain this statement.

A credit default swap insures a corporate bond issued by the reference entity against default. Its approximate effect is to convert the corporate bond into a risk-free bond. The buyer of a credit default swap has therefore chosen to exchange a corporate bond for a risk-free bond. This means that the buyer is long a risk-free bond and short a similar corporate bond.

Problem 23.18.
Why is there a potential asymmetric information problem in credit default swaps?

Payoffs from credit default swaps depend on whether a particular company defaults. Arguably some market participants have more information about this that other market participants (see Business Snapshot 23.2).

Problem 23.19.
Does valuing a CDS using real-world default probabilities rather than risk-neutral default probabilities overstate or understate its value? Explain your answer.

Real world default probabilities are less than risk-neutral default probabilities. It follows that the use of real world default probabilities will tend to understate the value of a CDS.

CHAPTER 24
Weather, Energy, and Insurance Derivatives

This chapter describes some non-traditional derivatives products. It considers how weather, energy, and insurance derivatives are typically structured.

The most common weather derivatives have payoffs dependent on the temperature at a particular weather station during a particular month. The temperature variable for a month is typically calculated as the cumulative cooling degree days (CDD) or cumulative heating degree days (HDD). The CDD for a day is max(A − 65, 0) where A is the average of the highest and lowest temperature in degrees Fahrenheit during the day. The HDD for a day is max(65 − A, 0). Popular contracts are forwards and options on the cumulative CDD or HDD during a month.

The three most important types of energy derivatives are oil derivatives, gas derivatives, and electricity derivatives. The oil derivatives market is a well-established market where a variety of different contracts (such as futures, forwards, swaps, and options) trade actively in both exchanges and over-the-counter markets. Contracts typically relate to the delivery of a certain number of gallons of a certain type of oil at a certain location. The gas derivatives market typically involves forward contracts or options for the delivery of gas at a certain rate to a certain hub for the whole of a month. The electricity derivatives contract also typically involves forward contracts or options for the delivery of electricity at a certain rate to a specific location for the whole of a month. However, in the case of electricity the supplier may have the right the change the rate at which power is supplied during the month in certain ways.

Energy prices exhibit volatility and mean reversion. This means that prices fluctuate randomly, but tend to be pulled back to a long-run average level. Oil has a relatively low volatility and a relatively low rate mean reversion. For gas the volatility and mean reversion are somewhat higher. Electricity has a very high volatility and a very high rate of mean reversion. (This is largely because storing electricity is difficult so that a day's demand must be met by electricity generation in that day.)

In a traditional reinsurance contract, an insurance company pays other companies to take on risks it does not want to bear itself. An alternative to traditional reinsurance is a CAT bond. CAT bonds typically offer a higher rate of interest than regular bonds. However, the bond principal may be used to pay insurance claims.

Answers to Practice Questions

Problem 24.8.
"HDD and CDD can be regarded as payoffs from options on temperature." Explain this statement.

HDD is $\max(65 - A, 0)$ where A is the average of the maximum and minimum temperature during the day. This is the payoff from a put option on A with a strike price of 65. CDD is $\max(A - 65, 0)$. This is the payoff from call option on A with a strike price of 65.

Problem 24.9.
Suppose that you have 50 years of temperature data at your disposal. Explain the analysis you would you carry out to calculate the forward cumulative CDD for next July.

It would be useful to calculate the cumulative CDD each July each year for the last 50 years. A linear regression relationship

$$CDD = a + bt + e$$

could then be estimated where a and b are constants, t is the time in years measured from the start of the 50 years, and e is the error. This relationship allows for linear trends in temperature through time. The expected CDD for next year (year 51) is then $a + 51b$. This could be used as an estimate of the forward CDD.

Problem 24.10.
Would you expect mean reversion to cause the volatility of the three-month forward price of an energy source to be greater than or less than the volatility of the spot price? Explain your answer.

The volatility of the three-month forward price will be less than the volatility of the spot price. This is because, when the spot price changes by a certain amount, mean reversion will cause the forward price will change by a lesser amount.

Problem 24.11.
Explain how a 5×8 option contract for May 2011 on electricity with daily exercise works. Explain how a 5×8 option contract for May 2011 on electricity with monthly exercise works. Which is worth more?

A 5×8 contract for May, 2011 is a contract to provide electricity for five days per week during the off-peak period (11pm to 7am). When daily exercise is specified, the holder of the option is able to choose each weekday whether he or she will buy electricity at the strike price at the agreed rate. When there is monthly exercise, he or she chooses once at the beginning of the month whether electricity is to be bought at the strike price at the agreed rate for the whole month. The option with daily exercise is worth more.

Problem 24.12.
Consider two bonds that have the same coupon, time to maturity, and price. One is a B-rated corporate bond. The other is a CAT bond. An analysis based on historical data shows that the expected losses on the two bonds in each year of their life are the same. Which bond would you advise a portfolio manager to buy and why?

The CAT bond has very little systematic risk. Whether a particular type of catastrophe occurs is independent of the return on the market. The risks in the CAT bond are likely to be largely "diversified away" by the other investments in the portfolio. A B-rated bond does have systematic risk that cannot be diversified away. It is likely therefore that the CAT bond is a better addition to the portfolio.

CHAPTER 25
Derivatives Mishaps and What We Can Learn From Them

Derivatives markets have been responsible for some spectacular losses. It is important to understand what went wrong and how similar catastrophes can be avoided in the future. This is the focus of this final chapter.

The most important point to understand is that derivatives can be used in many different ways. They can be used to reduce the risks that arise from a company's operations or to take risks. It is important for all companies (financial and nonfinancial) to define clear and unambiguous risk limits and to set up internal controls to ensure that the limits are adhered to.

It is hard to believe that some of the events outlined in this chapter actually happened. It is important to recognize that the events are not representative of how derivatives are used most of the time. Most derivatives trades are entered into for sensible reasons. Overall the derivatives industry has been a huge multi-trillion dollar success story. With the regulation that has been put in place since the crisis, it will be fascinating to see how it evolves in the years to come.